STITCHED

A Memoir

by
Marissa Carney

PublishAmerica
Baltimore

First printing

*For privacy and protection purposes, some names have been changed or omitted from this book.

ISBN: 1-4137-6001-5
PUBLISHED BY PUBLISHAMERICA, LLLP
www.publishamerica.com
Baltimore

Printed in the United States of America

Self-Mutilation: "Self-mutilation or self-injury is any form of self-harm inflicted on one's body without the intent to commit suicide."

Self-Mutilation is a real and actual illness that affects between two and four million people in the United States, mostly girls and women between their teenage years and early 30s.

More than 50 percent have been sexually abused. Many others are borderline personality or have dissociate or eating disorders.

The most common self-mutilation tactic is cutting one's skin with razors, knives, glass or other sharp objects. Cutting ranges from fairly superficial injuries to amputation.

Other self-injurious behavior includes burning, biting, bruising, hitting and pulling out body hair.

I remember clearly the first time I cut. That time, it was definitely meant to be suicidal.

But isn't it funny that I can't remember, just a few years later, cutting again? The one cut that set the precedence for a habit? One that could, and nearly did, kill me?

I was 16 or 17 the first time. I suppose it was all innocent enough.

Jamie was over for dinner before I had a dance program. I was not supposed to be dating Jamie, and I had, multiple times, told my mother we were just good friends and nothing more. That, of course, was a lie.

That night, Jamie and I were in the kitchen, lit only by the stove's overhead light, making macaroni and cheese before going together to the program. My mother was upstairs doing motherly things or whatever mothers do in their rooms.

Jamie and I thought we were alone enough to steal a few kisses.

But we were wrong. Very wrong.

My mother has a habit of sneaking up on a person when she thinks he or she is engaging in some sort of disagreeable behavior.

This time, she was right…but only in that I was engaging in disagreeable behavior in her opinion. I never thought anything about my relationship with Jamie was wrong, other than I had lied to her about it.

"Marissa. What in the hell are you doing?"

Those few words are ones I will never forget. I can't forget how they made me feel.

A clichéd "her words cut into me like a knife," could work, but it was more than that. My entire body went cold, then hot. Then numb. My stomach fell through the ground and straight down to hell. I felt as though I'd been stabbed. Time froze.

I turned around to face my mother. She stood there with a laundry basket on her hip, her face drawn and red, brown eyes almost a different color with anger.

I faced my mother. The only parent I had left. The only adult I could call mine. She was my everything; even being 16 and a typical teenager wanting privacy, independence and more rights, I knew that.

I'd lied to her and betrayed her. I didn't know what that would cost me. Our relationship as mother and daughter and the tentative relationship as friends we'd begun? Would she ever talk to me again? Pay for school, dance, clothes? Ever allow me to date? To go out with friends? Would she want to leave me as my father had? Would we ever be the same mom and daughter?

I was a good kid. Didn't drink, smoke, do drugs, party, sneak out or even lie much about anything. I got good grades, did extra-curricular things. To me, this was the end of all that. None of it mattered. Because of my selfishness and disrespect for authority, I'd lost it all, starting with my mother.

My mom was a good mom. Still is, as a matter of fact. She loves me and my older brother more than anything. She would do anything for us…and at that time, she was doing it all. Struggling to raise us and get us through school on her tiny salary, struggling to give us all the things we were used to having when we had two parents and some of the things we really wanted. And she never complained about it, at least to us or in such a way that we would feel responsible for her misery. Throughout that misery, she could forgive and love, no matter what.

I know that now. But when I was 16 or 17 and knew nothing about much, and she was my world, and I'd betrayed that, I felt lost, confused and scared to death.

So when Mom walked away, I picked up the knife I'd been using to cut Velveeta for the macaroni and cheese dinner. It was a small version of a butcher's cleaver, almost. Brown handle, wide, sharp blade.

I don't think I thought about it. I just did it. I managed to cut my left wrist a few times before Jamie wrestled the knife out of my grasp.

I didn't feel the cuts. They weren't very deep, but they bled. I remember looking at them and the blood, wondering where that power and instinct had come from to do that to myself. Looking at the cuts and thinking the blood was pretty.

Mom wasn't happy about that either. She didn't say much about it, other than something like, "So you didn't want to listen to your mom bitch, so you tried to kill yourself. That's smart." She never brought it up again. Neither did I; both of us brushing it off as just something that happened—teenage stuff.

As far as I'm concerned, it had no impact on the later years when I began to cut routinely. Somehow it all seemed so different.

The silence of that night's cutting remained as so for nearly nine more years.

Until one night, the culmination of years of cutting and hiding it, I cut deep enough to need 25 stitches.

Then it all came out, just like the blood I'd grown to need come out of me, the basic story behind it all came out to my mother.

Most everything else remained written down in my journals. My thoughts and feelings, moods, just about everything that led up to that night. The things I didn't want to or wasn't ready to share with her or many other people.

I've always wondered what I would do with all my old journals. Full of random, useless observations and stories, full of my deepest, rawest, most un-edited emotions.

On my journey through all of this, I would sometimes share things I'd written with a small group of friends. Three girlfriends from work who had gotten involved with my struggles and swore they'd see me through until I got better. To me and my counselor at the time, they became known as the "Save Marissa Coalition."

I wanted them to be able to talk to me and I to them. But I'm not the greatest talker, especially about myself. I know they felt awkward about asking me questions or bringing up the subject of cutting. As my way around all of that, I'd type up some paragraphs from my journal and email them to the girls.

One of the friends said she could see me using my experiences to help others some day. Then another one said the same thing. Then the third. They couldn't *all* be off base.

At the time, I was already working on two "novels," both of which touched on what I was going through. One was fiction, loosely based on me. The other was non-fiction about a variety of topics, and I

9

wasn't sure I could mix it with cutting. Especially to the depth cutting deserves.

So, I thought…and thought some more. How could I write a book to help others either understand self-mutilation or perhaps overcome it? I'm not an expert. I'm just someone who went through it all, and someone who had most of it documented.

The light clicked, and there it was.

And so here it is.

These are the journalings I could find. Something of a beginning, semblances of a middle and an ending I'll probably still be working long after this hits the shelves, if ever it does.

I used to scour websites and libraries in search of books on self-mutilation. Usually all I ever found were books written by doctors for counselors, which were of little help to me. The medical language was tough to get through. I didn't care how a counselor could get into my head and help me deal….*I* wanted to get into my head and help myself deal. I got on a lot of websites and into a lot of chat rooms and read up about it. I found that most of them centered on people who were still cutting themselves, not trying to quit. Reading about those people who still were made me want to do it all the more, not stay away from it. I wanted a first-hand account of others who went through the same thing—why they did this, how they found help and got through it—that sort of thing.

So, what if someone else out there is going through the same thing I was? If someone comes across this book written by me, and it helps them, the passion I've had to write since I could form letters into words is all for a purpose.

I've always wondered what my purpose in life is.

The entries span years. From 1999 on. Some are months apart either because I was too messed up to pick up a pen, or I just didn't feel like writing. Some are long and detailed, even disturbing. Even to me, and I'm the one who was doing it all. Some entries don't make sense.

The pieces of the story mesh to make a whole. In between some of the entries, I write more. To expand, to detail, to get it all out. So you understand and so you find the answers you're looking for or for some that you didn't even know had questions.

I add family background and stories.

I add poetry and short stories I've written along the way.

I add the people I've met, the things they've said to me and done for me.

I add the things I've learned.

I add random thoughts I thought that still make me laugh or make me sad when I read them all these years later.

I add suggestions, regrets, wishes and plans for the future.

It's all in here. What one could call the ultimate journal of my life. The ultimate journal of the largest struggle in my life.

October 4, 1999
What is my purpose for being on this earth? Do I have one?

October 12
I wonder if it's sad that I've never really had a positive male role model. Then again, what defines positive? And is that really going to matter much in the future? Am I really going to turn into some crazy maniac all because of my [father figures]?

October 27
I work and I try to so hard to do things right and well…why do I always seem to still not be number one?

November 17
I cannot stand not being perfect.

December 24
In a moment of quiet self-reflectance…I have so much to be thankful for. And I am. I truly am. I don't feel as though I deserve it, though. I don't feel like a good person. But sometimes I do. But when I really think about it, I don't feel as though I am. What can I do to become a better person? Be nice to everybody? Be nicer to certain people? Do more for others, help others more, think nicer thoughts.

I want to be a better person. Perhaps these should be some new year's resolutions.

January 11, 2000
Maybe someday I'll have life's answer. What is life's question? Does life have one? If it does have one, do I really want to know it? Do I really want all the answers?

January 24
What the hell am I going to do with all these books and journals? I don't think I'm very comfortable having other people read some of the things I've written during my life.

January 25
I am always confused. I'm thinking too much today, and I wonder why. Am I smart? Am I pretty? Am I good enough? Stop thinking!

***

Those are some the warm-up entries. They kind of set the stage for future entries, setting up how I felt about myself and my abilities.

I was always a loud, outgoing, unshy kid. I had a lot of friends, though I was never in the "A group," never really fit in anywhere in particular. I took my share of jibes and rude comments throughout junior and senior high school about my face, my clothing, my social status, my sexuality. I realized then that I wasn't much of anything. I learned how mean people could be. I found out that all of my good qualities I thought I had didn't mean shit. That could be when my self-esteem issues began and surged.

I probably began cutting first as punishment. When I hit college, I'm not sure I had much self-worth left in me.

I made a couple of friends, did a few things on campus, joined the dance team. But I preferred to be alone most of the time, or in the company of just one or two people. I constantly compared myself to everyone else. I wasn't pretty enough, thin enough, smart enough, fast enough, funny, intense or outgoing enough, reserved enough, demure enough, *anything* enough. Even though I pulled off a 4.0 grade point average my first two years of college and finished with an overall 3.89… even though I weighed a normal amount and held down multiple jobs, once as many as three, and was on the university's dance team… even though I could have probably dated anyone I wanted in college…I still wasn't perfect.

On the surface, I was happy with my life, I guess. I loved the freedom of college, loved the autonomy and felt happy working as hard as I did. I had close friends, liked my major (communications with a minor in dance) and all of my jobs (dance teacher/gymnastics coach, radio DJ and babysitter).

So what was the big deal? How much better could I get?

I never found out that answer, and cutting was my punishment for it.

I cut my arms and wrists for getting lower grades than I thought I would get, for hurting someone's feelings, for not putting 150 percent into every project I did, every dance I choreographed, every paper I wrote.

I was never good enough, so there was always a reason to cut.

By anyone else's standards, I pushed myself beyond the norm. I put too much pressure on myself, but I couldn't see that at the time. I thought I didn't go far *enough*.

I only saw the criticisms for not going to enough parties on campus, or not rushing a stupid sorority. I saw the criticisms for not loosening up and letting go. Years of being told I was too sensitive made me even more sensitive. I was constantly told that I was too hard to talk to because I was so sensitive and took everything wrong way.

I saw that I would never be what everyone wanted me to be. I wasn't good enough for myself. I wasn't good enough for anyone else either. And so, I, quite literally, cut myself down for being who I was and who I wasn't.

***

13

January 25

There's something quite powerful about cutting your own wrist and watching the blood drain out. Knowing that you did that....it's your own blood, your own life and you're controlling it. Wow.

I hate myself. I'm pretty good from hiding that from other people. But I think I'm better at hiding it from myself.

***

That's how the first entry I could find specifically about cutting goes. I have no idea what prompted those words, what situation I was in at the time, why I was cutting. It was daring to write them in the first place, no matter how cryptic.

I've always been protective of my journals, always afraid someone would get a hold of them and read them. Especially during my college years, when those kinds of entries became typical.

I was especially terrified of my mother going through them, so I always kept them with me in my school bag or hidden in my room. Even then, I was suspicious she'd try to find them in there too.

One day in college, I did catch her shuffling through one, the one with the stars and moons on it. She'd taken it out of my bag while she thought I was out. I snuck upstairs with the suspicion of what she was doing. I just had a feeling. Just as I'd betrayed her trust with Jamie, she betrayed mine with my privacy.

Lucky for me at that point, she didn't find anything that would have given me away.

She told me she was worried about me, and because I never talked to her anymore, she thought she'd find out what was wrong with me by reading my journals. Certainly not something that was never attempted by any other parent in the past. Certainly something I can understand, but can't agree with.

Back then, I can't imagine having been ready to share any of this with anyone, especially my mother. It took me years longer to let her in and even then, I'm not sure I was ready. I was kind of forced to do it.

After we got that little episode out of the way, my entries became more detailed...thinking she wouldn't risk trying to sneak in a read again. My journal was my lifeline, my sanity, my greatest weapon with which to get through each day. My entries became bolder and more detailed. More real and true. What's a journal if you can't be honest in it?

Now I'm ready to share it.

***

January 26
Where is hell? Where is heaven? Which will I be in? Probably hell. I'm not worth anything else.

January 28
I think I would have been ok if that car had hit me. I mean, I don't think I would have minded much. At this point, who cares?

That's my blood. Why can't I just do it? In my heart, I know it's wrong, I guess. But I deserve to hurt. I deserve to bleed. I deserve to die.

February 9
I think these headaches are a form of punishment from God. So, even though it hurts like hell, it's good pain because I deserve it. I need to see some blood. I am not proud of myself now or of my past. I'm afraid to die, yet thinking about it is so comforting. When I am dead, maybe I'll never have to think again. Won't have to remember anything...won't have to hide anything. Maybe when I'm dead, I won't have to hate myself anymore.

February 14
Blood is my color,
On my hands, in my mouth.
Red looks good on me,
Bleeding me into life.

***

There are a lot of reasons why people cut…or burn or pick or pull or hit themselves with whatever method of self-harm they choose.

For me, it started out as one thing: punishment. Then it became sort of a catch-all.

All of that literature I've read backs up my reasons. I guess that makes me feel a little better—less of a freak. There are reasons why I, why we, do this. By we, I mean, not just me. I was never naive enough to think I was alone in this.

No, I wasn't alone in what I did, but I *felt* alone—just because that's how it is for depressives, self-mutilators and just about anyone at different times in their lives, right? Who could understand what I was going through and feeling? What normal person would really want to? I didn't know anyone else who was a cutter, and when I did find someone who used to be, she kind of got immersed in her own problems and faded out from my life. I met a trichotillomaniac (a hair-puller), later on after I'd already stopped cutting.

I don't remember when I started cutting as a coping technique. Maybe I blocked it out or "dissociated" at the time. I don't even remember the second time I cut to feel better. It just suddenly came into my life like it was always there, and I always did it.

I know that I told myself lies for a long time. I told myself there wasn't anything wrong with me. I told myself that I could quit anytime I wanted. I could admit I had issues, so I didn't really try to do anything about them for a really long time. Sure, I had issues, but who didn't?

I told myself that what I was doing wasn't bad. It was just something I never noticed anyone else around me doing. I wrote in my journals that it was abnormal and odd because I knew other people would think of it that way. They wouldn't understand it. My doctors told me that should have been my first clue that cutting wasn't healthy—knowing no one else would look at it as such.

It wasn't odd to me in my heart and in my head. It was just part of everyday life that I wrote in my journals about, much like I wrote about not wanting to do a group project or go to work. I was dissociated from it, not fully understanding it—too close to see it for what it really was.

I don't remember why I thought cutting would be a good idea, how I thought it would help. By the time I did know what I was doing and for what reasons, it was too late—I was hooked.

It is an addiction, just like any other. One that, like any other, becomes an obsession and one that can kill you.

One and the Other

One side watches

    (as the other one bleeds,
    slip slides into absence)

Stoic with a smile
No, nothing is wrong

    (I just can't breathe)

One of them dies
so the other can live

    (Hiding under red,
    suicide with no consequence)

The sacrifice of one
And the other watches

    (I just turn away)

6/24/04 – 7/1/04

February 20
Red looks good on me. Blood is my color, on my hands, in my face.
I don't like that.
Red is my color worn on my deserving body, blood looks good on me, running from my wrists, filling up my hands.
That's better.

February 23
I have an obsession with blood.

March 3
Red is my color
Worn on my deserving body
Blood looks good on me
Running from my wrists
Filling up my hands

March 4
Could something really be wrong with me?

March 5
What *is* the secret of life? Is there such a thing? I guess it's just what people make of it.
I think I have a serious mental problem.

March 7
I feel angry, sad, depressed, exhausted, tired and very alone right now. Something has to give, but I don't know what or how I can.
I feel myself falling back to that darkness—I don't want to get there again because I don't know if I could get myself out again.
I wonder if I could be a manic-depressive.

Insanity

Locked within my mind,
There is only so much I can do—
Or say, or see, or hear.
There is only so much I can wish—
The empty voids where love once was.
This fear that has become tangled
And taken over my thoughts
Leaves me hanging by a finger—
A tiny grip on what life once was.

Insanity sets me free,
But locks me inside my mind.
I see my thoughts as ghosts that form
To haunt me of past breaths.
I smell the death, so heavy upon me,
An imminent death—
I'm lost.

What is to be done
As patterns of characters
Set themselves free within me?
Where can I go,
Which tunnel is mine,
Which way shall be my last?

March 14
Along with being a manic-depressive, I believe I'm also an insomniac or something. I do not need to sleep. I am wide-awake at all times.

March 15
I wonder why this cut didn't scar on my wrist.

March 19
I did it again last night. I don't even think I know when I'm doing it anymore. I'd be concerned if it were anybody else, I guess. But not me.
    I wonder if I could really need some sort of…I hate the word "counseling." I don't think it's for wusses or anything. Of course not. But I also don't want to admit I need help when I don't know if I do. If I had to decide right now, I'd say no. But maybe I'm just saying that because I don't know any better. But I don't know why I do anything I do that's probably considered "abnormal." Maybe that's just how I am. But if [a friend of mine] did something like that, I don't know what I'd do. Certainly not think she was normal. I'd be sad and wouldn't want to think of her doing that. But I guess she wouldn't because she's…smarter, stable. Sane.
    But I am too. I think. Sometimes I have no idea. All I know is I have some severe issues with myself. I think it's a good thing I can at least admit I have "issues." Now the question is how should I fix them? I don't have an answer.

March 29
I'm not doing too well right now. I feel very…crazy, I guess is a good word.
    It's a good thing I'm too tired to go down to the kitchen. Otherwise who knows what would happen.

March 30
Manic-depression. I think I had another "episode."

It's really nice when I forget about how much I hate myself. Perhaps that's why I feel safest around other people—they make me forget.

If only for a few moments.

To dance upon moonbeams
Is to find my deepest strength
To feel my hidden pride and
To see an outward beauty
That is who I really am.

I actually have a smile right now. I can't believe those words came from my own hand. I like the sound of them. They give me hope that maybe someday the words will come true.

I saw my life tonight,
Touched it, held it,
Wondered that something so pretty
Could be within that which is too ugly
To be free.

March 31
I saw my life tonight,
Touched it held it,
Wondered that something so pretty
Could be within that which is too ugly
To ever be free
My life's color, so brilliant against
Pale skin
It's brilliant color

Let Me Bleed.

Let Me Bleed

I see my blood,
Touch it, hold it,
Wonder that something so pretty
Is actually a part of me,
Comes from within me.
I watch my blood, red from violation and penetration
Roll away from the razor blade's cut.
Pain and hurt slide from my arms
Leaving streaks of failure and fuck-up;
I wear these words so well.

This is what's right for me,
This is what I deserve,
Just let me bleed.

I drag the blade through my skin
Praying for strength to go deeper,
Praying for my veins to open up,
Hating myself because they won't.
Hating myself for doing it,
But fascinated by its addictiveness
And the power I hold in my own hand.

It may be what I've chosen,
But it's also what I deserve,
Just let me bleed.

Blood has always fascinated me. No specific reason why, it just has. I don't panic or get sick at the sight of other people's blood. I've seen a lot of it just from some of the stories I've covered. It captivates me when it's pooled on the roadway or smeared across the window of a car. That used to be *inside* somebody else; it's what made them alive, what made them breathe. It's those times that I wish I could scoop it up in my hands and put it back inside the person and make her whole again.

I wonder what it would be like to try to stop someone else from bleeding to death, because then I'd be touching it, practically immersed in it.

I could stare at my wrists for hours, looking at the blue veins, wondering what's really coursing through them. Is it really blue until air hits it and makes it red? That red color that nothing else can replicate.

Then I wonder why blood changes to that rusty red color when it dries, which is pretty in itself, but nothing like fresh blood is.

That nothing else feels like or smells like. It's just beautiful to me.

The most beautiful part of me.

It's life; tangible.

There are different kinds of blood, too. Paper cut blood is thin and slow to come to the surface.

Shaving nicks are long, but bubble up in the middle, then just run, no matter how much you blot at them.

Hang nail blood wells up, then drips in long, steady streams.

Knife cuts are a mixture, depending on what kind of knife you use. Your skin follows the pattern of the knife, and doesn't seem to break open right away. It kind of pauses for a moment, deciding what to do, then reluctantly rises.

Razor blade cuts...the most precise of the cuts. There's no stopping that blood. Your skin parts immediately, and the blood rushes out, like water behind a dam that's broken. And with it, what you think is your pain.

***

April 1

I've come to the conclusion that I really do suck at everything. I cannot do anything right. Or even good. It all is terrible.

Life is so precious and so full of wonderful things. I know this, but I don't know how I'm supposed to just snap out of how I'm feeling. I would love to. There's nothing more I'd like than to be my "happy" self all the time. But under that, how can I be truly happy when I'm not? This isn't what I want for myself, but I don't know how to be who I want. I don't know how to fix myself—to make myself happy.

I don't know how to just forget about harsh words I've come to accept as true, how to forget about hating myself and instead become the real Marissa I know is still around somewhere. I don't know how to get over my feeling of inadequacy, ugliness….I don't know how to realize maybe I can't do everything as well as other people, but that I can still do it in my own way and style. How do I convince myself that yes, someone will want me and I will want them right back more than anyone else? How do I tell myself I'm worth something, anything? I'm not a terrible person. I have good qualities and a smile no one can look away from.

How do I get over the things I've done in my life that I shouldn't have?

How do I let go of everything I've ever done, thought of myself, condemned myself for, the past and the present.

I could do what I've always had in mind. I could kill myself. It would be easy. I hate myself that much. But at the same time, I want to prove to myself I can be okay. I can learn how to do all the things I've written about. I can be a good person, I can like who I am, what I'll become. I'm sure I can be better than I think I am. I can make people, make myself, proud.

I just want to *live*. I want to find someone to marry, a few kids to love me for a while. I want to excel in my job. I want to travel and see the world, I want to be free.

Free.

That word means so much. It's the light at the end of a long tunnel. I'm at one end—it's at the other. I want to get to that end so much. God, please, help me…to just be free.

***

That's how it goes most of the time. It's like a constant struggle between two, sometimes three of me.

There's the me I think I am underneath all of this skin and all of this sadness and hurt; the me that comes out every now and then that I wish I could be all the time—the funny, fun, adventurous, silly, spontaneous, pretty me; the one I write about being beautiful and strong and who dances so close to heaven.

Then there's the other me. The me who is so uncertain, a perfectionist with low self-esteem, who feels guilty and bad about everything all of the time; the me who feels like an outcast and loser, who's too sensitive and perceives things wrong all of the time; the me who isn't intelligent enough, thin enough, fast enough, perfect enough; the me who wants to hurt herself and make herself bleed.

Some days I feel completely like one—the next, I totally feel like the other. I feel like I have multiple personality disorder. Only I know I can't because I'm aware of these two Marissas battling over mind and heart. Sometimes I want to shoot them both.

It's tough to nail down exactly why I have felt this way to such an extreme. I know everyone feels split at times, but, apparently, it's not normal when you start cutting yourself over it.

It's tough to say how or when I got to be this way, exactly. I'm not sure any of this was an issue when I was not yet in the double digits. Maybe I just don't remember. Maybe it's just something that develops in some later in life.

Hmmmmmmm. Maybe this is why I'm not in the psychotherapy field.

It's annoying to be two people—or three, as the case may be, when you're *pretending* to be person number one to hide everything that's hurting you just to placate everyone so they want to be your friend and don't get annoyed or sick of you.

In my heart, I've always wanted to be person number one. I could always see her, feel her, hear her. I liked her because she *was* me. When she went away, it was like looking at her through a pond's reflection and not being able to reach her, touch her or breathe her in.

Spending most of my time as person number two or three hurt even more because it wasn't really me—and I knew it. I just wanted me back so badly.

For some reason, I couldn't get there. The depression and bad feelings were so much stronger, and I don't know if I'll ever figure out why. Perhaps because I spent so much time being the *dark one* that it was simply more comfortable there. Badness just sucks you in sometimes, and like quicksand, the more you struggle and want out, the deeper in you get.

It's sad for me to look back and think about all the fun things I missed out on, all the years I lost to just be me. Not because I really chose to, but because it couldn't be helped. A lot of times I was too depressed to enjoy my time out at activities. I was too self-conscious, sad or upset about something. People can't help the way they feel, no matter how much someone else wants them to.

One of the things that's sometimes hard to deal with while dealing with self-mutilation is how other people see you and interact with you.

I knew my friends cared a great deal through everything, lowest points to highest. All three were constantly calling me at home; Trisha, even setting her alarm for two or three in the morning, knowing I would still be up. I got a lot of cards and little knickknack things. They would all pull me aside and ask how I was doing, prod, convince and encourage me to get into counseling, give hugs, remind me they loved me….and even organized an "intervention" dinner one night. A time where I could talk openly about what I was going through and what I needed from them. Complete with lasagna, plenty of chocolate and a basket full of coping tools. Band-Aids, extra-strength Neosporin, journals so I would write instead of cut, a bracelet to wear on my left wrist so I would think of them when I struggled with a razor, hugs, Hershey Kisses…incredible friends— the kind there aren't enough of… the kind I never thought I deserved to have. The kind I felt guilty over because I did have them.

They were usually nothing but understanding and supportive…to my face. I know that Amy once said she wanted to slap me around, then lock me in the basement until I came to my "senses."

I'm sure I was frustrating, unresponsive at times. I know I hurt their feelings and made them cry and worry. I drove them nuts and gave them nothing in return.

But still they stood by me, even though I did come close to blowing it all.

It was a learning stage for them, though, I'm sure. Just how *do* you deal with a freak?

I imagine they handled me the way I handle others with problems. As I'm sure anyone can attest to, problems get old after awhile. You get tired of saying the same things over and over to the same person with the same problem. Eventually, you start screening your phone calls, making excuses not to do things with the person, turn and walk the other way when he or she is coming toward you.

It hurts to think my coalition ever did that, though maybe they didn't. The point is, nobody quite understands what's happening. As much as they let you cry and talk and rant and rave, they wonder why you can't just get it together. Just shape up, be okay and move on. I think it's too hard for them to realize you just can't. It's like trying to stop breathing on purpose—impossible.

Being depressed or being a self-mutilator isn't something one can just stop. It's all so deep inside, embedded, ingrained, a part of you. It's sometimes too scary to let out and let go. It's a habit, compulsion. There is simply no other way to explain it.

You just can't stop.

People who don't live it can't comprehend that. It can be hurtful when they don't comprehend that they don't comprehend. Comprende?

Before "Hospital Night," my friends didn't always come to me and ask me all the questions they wanted to. Trisha told me they were just afraid to approach me, afraid of pushing me over the edge by being too nosy. After Hospital Night, she told me nobody knew what to say to me, or how to ask if I was doing okay. After the first few days, it seemed like they were ignoring me, trying to put the episode aside, like it never happened. Everyone walked on eggshells around me, and I hated that. I wanted them to come to me if they had questions, if they needed to talk about it. I wanted to feel like I could go to them too. They promised they wouldn't leave me, but it started to feel like they were.

Communication broke down, and it was really hard on me.

The first few days after the incident were some of the worst in my whole life. I was dealing with what I'd done to myself and to some of my dearest friends. They were all mad at me, and I wasn't sure I could even call them friends anymore. My mother came up to my apartment to be with me day and night, so I was doing a lot of talking and explaining, which was stressful. I had to call off work for a whole week, knowing people were talking about me, knowing I would have to talk to my boss at some point and explain some things to him. I started on an anti-depressant called Effexor. Until it got in my system, it messed with my head. I couldn't eat, I slept, but fitfully and was even more depressed when I woke up.

Everything was a mess, and I then truly wanted to be dead. I wasn't sure anything would ever be the same again, and I wasn't sure I had the strength to try and put it all back together.

My mother was an angel to me, trying to understand as best she could. She listened to everything I had to say and wasn't judgmental. She didn't tell me I was right or wrong. She didn't yell at me or make me feel bad.

My friends were a bit different. I'm sure because they'd already been through so much and were so damn sick of it all. They were frustrated, angry and tired. They were hurt, sad and disappointed. And they were mad about how it all went down. Which I'll get to later, but my point is, I don't think they could have possibly understood. They thought maybe I did it on purpose, that I could have helped myself or whatever.

But that's just not true.

I need to point that out. Because again, this can't be compared to, say, talking yourself out of buying a new pair of shoes or something.

I think some of the most hurtful things that came out of the whole incident were things my friends said to me and about me.

I made a point of talking to each person directly involved after it all happened.

Jennifer, who was on the list, called me selfish.

Amy was on the list, as well.

On the drive home from Virginia, where it all happened, I spoke with her briefly on my cell phone. She called me after Trisha called her to let her know what happened. As soon as I answered, she said, "I love you."

I started crying. I may have whispered something like, "Hi, thank you."

She just said it again. "I love you." Words that always make me melt coming from someone I care so much about.

When I talked face to face with her a few days later, it somehow wasn't the same. She was cold and distant. Hell-bent on making me see what an ass I was and how wrong I was.

Then she called me manipulative and obsessive.

My heart stopped.

Just imagine one of your best friends telling you that you are those things, in complete seriousness. At a time you probably needed her the most.

I'm already sensitive to begin with. Plus, I was on new drugs. I had black yarn stuff sticking out of my arm. My life was a mess. Then to be called manipulative and obsessive. I wasn't either of those things.

She was just a little off track. Amy, Trisha, Jenny, Mom...nobody in the world could truly comprehend that. They could just make up conclusions in their minds to suit themselves so they would feel better. Like maybe I was something concrete to fix. Then I could be okay and leave them all alone.

It doesn't work like that, though. Much as I wish it could.

Another thing that hurt too, was a second comment of Amy's, "I don't want to say it....but we told you so."

Now, what was that supposed to do for me? I was already feeling as horrible as a person really can, I already knew that things got out of hand. They exploded when I thought they wouldn't. Nobody likes to be reminded of that, and there wasn't any need for her to say that. Was it revenge? Was it just to make me feel worse than I already did? Was I supposed to break down in tears and proclaim my friends' amazing insight? Proclaim their ability to tell the future? Grovel and say, "You were so right. I will never doubt you again?" Maybe it was just something she felt she really needed to say. Maybe it just slipped out.

Since the day Amy said that to me, the only thing I really planned on doing on the year "anniversary" of not cutting? Writing Amy a simple email.

Amy-
It's been a year.
I told you so.
-Marissa

Amy always doubted that I would never cut again. She didn't think that March night would be the last time. She didn't think I could do it. Some days, even I didn't think I could—but I would be damned if I was going to prove her right.

It hurt to know even my best friends didn't believe in me. I guess I was hoping for some other reaction—maybe a little more support, a little more trust. Something like, "Well, I'm still here for you." Or maybe I was just being unrealistic. I couldn't completely blame them for their reactions after putting them through so much.

I think as time wore on, I became really defensive about what happened that night and about me and the way they all saw me. Amy told me once that actions speak louder than words. After a while, I started to feel under intense scrutiny for anything I did, anything I said, every single facial expression I made. I felt like they were all looking for anything to call me on just because they were all still mad at me. I started to feel like I couldn't talk to anyone anymore because they didn't want to hear it, no matter how much "it" was hurting me. It seemed to me that any emotion I had, whatever I was feeling, was wrong to everyone else. I shouldn't be mad, or sad, or irritated or hurt. I should just feel like everyone else felt about my situations, I should just get a grip, grow up, do anything but feel how I felt and be who I was.

I had been hiding my feelings from everyone for so long, even myself, that for once, I really just wanted to feel. Nobody would let me. I ended up being really bitter about that. Then, I took to heart something my mom says a lot. "You feel how you feel, and that's okay."

It *is* okay to feel. All my life I've been told I'm too sensitive too defensive. So, of course, I'm going to feel that way. Automatically. Everyone says it, so it must be true. How could I not feel defensive and sensitive about being defensive and sensitive? How could I not feel sad and guilty about feeling that way? No one can say, "Okay, time's up, start feeling better about yourself." I have to be the one to let it all go, whenever I'm ready. What's not okay, though, is letting it go on for too long.

What I try to do now is feel, rationalize it, then compartmentalize it. Then let it go. There is no point in carrying it with me everywhere I go because there is always something else out there to worry about or give some thought to—some other emotion that needs to be put in its place.

I've forgiven (if you want to call it that) my friends for some of the things that came out of their mouths. Whether they believed in me or not at the time, it doesn't matter now. It may have made me that much stronger.

I certainly don't remember only the harsh, hurtful words. When I look at my friends, I don't see the trying times we've been through or, the sad tears we've shed. I simply see them—their beauty and their souls.

Their concern and their hearts and their love are all I could ever hope to have.

Deeper Than You Know

I cannot help the way I am
Life and circumstance have made me
This way
Everyone says that's okay
Until they disagree
Nobody is ever happy with
Anyone or anything
What kind of humanity is that?
Take a look inside yourself and
Fix what's wrong there
We're all deeper than we think
And I'm deeper than you know.

Whatever I feel is wrong,
So why should I feel at all
My actions speak differently to everybody
They see what they want
So why do I keep acting at all
I can talk
But don't say anything to bring us down,
Too mean or too sad too wrong or too true
I don't want to talk at all anymore
Because I'm deeper than you know
And you just won't look.

Nothing is skin-deep
I'm rarely what you think
And all your analyzing, gossip and rumors
Just make me fit your mold
But my soul, my soul won't be sold.
For you.

Look at yourself
And decide who you are
Before you even guess who I am,
Look inside yourself,
Fix what's wrong there
We're all deeper than we think
And I'm deeper than you know.

April 4
It was weird hearing her talk about her roommate like that. "She purposefully hurts herself." My face probably became quite red. It's weird to think there are other people who do those kinds of things. I wonder what was running through [my friend's] mind.

I wish I could take away everyone's pain. If I could, but then felt it all on myself, I think I would do it anyway.

I really do love life. I think I always have. I mean, how can I not? Is it possible to love life and be suicidal at the same time?

Oh, Lord. I thought I was okay for a minute there; however, I am not. Honestly, I thought I was having a nervous breakdown today. I wonder, really, if I'd know for sure. I think the one I had last week some time was a baby one. It was pretty scary.

I watched my blood
Dance away from the razor blade's cut

April 6
I've gone for 3 whole days without cutting myself. Minor accomplishments.

I watched my blood
Dance away from the razor blade's cut
A dance of pain, a dance of hurt,
A dance of sweet release

April 11
"We really can't love anyone until we love ourselves, first."

I think that line is a bunch of crap. If anything, I think hating yourself makes a person love everyone else all the more. I think it helps fill in the spot of myself that's empty. I like loving other people.

Besides, saying, "Oh, I love myself" is so gay. I guess it's okay to *like* yourself—who you are as a person and all that. But even that sounds ridiculous. Do I envy the people who do like themselves, though? I don't know. It's probably nice to think you're a good person and think you have good qualities. But it's just as good to hate yourself, then turn away from the mirror and go try to love others even more. I think when you don't like yourself, you spend more time thinking about other people—and that's a nice thing.

April 12
It's a toss up right now; go to bed or give in to these tears.
What is wrong with me?
I'm fucked up. FUCKED UP.

April 18
A prayer:
God—I know I haven't been anywhere near devout or deserving of a place in Your heart. I'm sorry that I use my energies on much smaller things than You. I don't know how to bring You back into my life, but I know I have to find a way.

Please look not upon my sins, but on me as a very tired, confused and lost young woman. I need to feel Your love, and I need You to help me find my way from darkness and into Your eternal light.

April 19
One of the worst days of my life was when I found out I couldn't give blood anymore.

May 4
Blood. Bleed.
I'd love to bleed it all out. Everything—just have it bleed right out of me.
How to make it through "safely." I wish I knew.
It's weird to think of the time and energy I spend worrying that other people are worrying too. It never occurred to me that [a friend] "worries" about me. I don't know if that should make me feel good…or just worry that she worries. I don't think I'm worth anybody worrying over, really.

May 13
These past few days have really proven to me just what a fucking

bitch I really am.

Oh, my God. Every nice thing I've ever done, ever will do, does not make up for who I am. I can't stand myself.

Maybe that's why I like looking at pictures of myself—that girl in the picture is not really me. She's who I'd like to be. Either just that smiling face or just a picture. That's all that should be of me. A picture.

May 27

I think I have multiple personalities.

If I were dead, would I be happy?

It's interesting to read my old journals from junior high and see that then I was pretty unhappy too. On the inside, anyway.

I need to die.

June 6

Sex is degrading to a woman when she's on the bottom, I think.

Then again, I tend to think sex is degrading all together.

Perhaps this sounds....I don't know the word for it; I don't even know what I want to say, really. I don't know if I look forward to the day I don't think that anymore or not. I don't know if I ever will not think that. I wonder if anyone else thinks how I do.

Sex is something that just baffles me, and most of the time I wish I could just see it as a normal person...or at least someone other than myself since I'm not sure what a normal person is. I wish I could see it as someone who's, like, had it, I guess and then, of course, as someone who hasn't.

It's hard to imagine that it can be a non-violent, non-degrading act that is out of love. The thought is, like, absolutely foreign to me.

June 7

"You bleed faster if you cut this way."

June 9

There are so many things I wish I could get over, things I wish I could forget I'd done and said...I feel sad that I have regrets in my life. Already. I'm just 22...I shouldn't have any. Yet I have so many. And that hurts me so deeply.

When we drove past the Catholic cemetery today, I felt like St. Matthew was reaching out for me...his arms open to take me into them, erase everything from me. It was like he was saying to me "Come on, precious. You belong here with me."

It was so strange and even now, all these hours later, I can still feel that so strongly.

June 20
Today's earlier scene, admittedly made me think a lot, but I don't think it made me change my mind about death.

What would, if not that? It scared me. But more for the fear of other people dying.

July 9
I think, just maybe, I'm beginning to mesh into one person. It's weird to think that since I've been two or three separate Marissas for so long. Or maybe that's just based on how I feel right now.

Maybe I'm healing—although I'm not sure that's possible.

July 10
I worry I may lose part of myself by "healing," though. I mean, I'm "me" because of what's happened in my life so far...I think, anyway. And sometimes that annoys me. Why can't I be the way I am just because I am? Or maybe I am and I just don't know it.

I'm a perfectionist because I have to be to counter all the things I tell myself.

July 12
I don't think I'm "healing" like I thought I was. But I think I've accepted the fact that I won't heal, and that's okay because it's a part of me. If that makes sense.

July 13
I'm a terrible person, and I hate myself and if I die right now, I can't imagine anything else that would be better.
I could find a gun.
I could do the wrists.
I could take some pills.
I could stand in front of a train…a car…a bus.
I could take a jump.
I could take a swim.
I could….just die.
Run my car into a tree, run it into the river.
I would want my mom to have….well, I guess she'd have everything anyway. But I think I'd want her to keep close to her my blanket, the angel statue she got me and the mouse music box where they're all dancing around the mirror.
I want [a friend] to have all the notes from high school I still have. The dance picture she gave me. She should have Bonnie. My Bee Gee's lunch box and *Saturday Night Fever* poster. She can have any jewelry she made for me too.
[My brother] would maybe want my *X-Files* posters and Enigma CDs. All my tie-dyed shirts. My Lionel Cabbage Patch Kid. My *Winnie the Pooh* book he gave me.
I guess everyone else could just pick out what they want if anything because I'm too tired to come up with anything for them.
[A friend] could have all my whale stuff. A tie-dye. Her poems she wrote for me. My opal ring. My fish tank. The Prince of Egypt. That cowboy hat magnet.

Here is my gun
Silver and new
When I put it to my head,
What will you do?
Close my eyes,
It will be so quick,
Russian roulette,
Just one will do the trick.
First bullet blank,
I won't stop it with one,
Second shot hollow,
Won't stop till it's done.
No luck with a third try.
Now we're half way through,
When I put it in my mouth,
What will you do?
A fourth explosion
But I'm not worried,
The right one will come,
Death won't be hurried.
Let's do it again
It's becoming quite fun,
One more blank—
There, now we're done.
Just one to go,
A last bullet of lead
Lodged down my throat,
And I will be dead.
Here is my gun
Silver and new,
When I pull the trigger,
What will you do?

revised 4/19/01

I have done my fair share of thinking about suicide. For a while, I thought it was really because I did want to die. I mean, I did really want to for a time. But later, I think that wasn't the case anymore. I wanted to live, I just didn't know how and was too afraid, and thoughts about suicide were just so compelling. I believe everyone thinks about it from time to time for whatever reasons.

For me, thinking about killing myself was the fantasy that kept me from thinking about all the hurt inside me. And maybe even from actually doing it. It was fantasy, something to run to, something I knew I could control—my fantasies. I could also control the suicide if I chose. The time, the method, everything about it.

I reveled in the details of fantasy. And that's hard to explain why playing it all out in your head is more fulfilling than actually trying anything. I guess because once you actually kill yourself, you're done and can't plan more ways to do it. There's a certain comfort in killing yourself over and over, when you're like me or the other thousands, millions of us who dream of it.

You dream of holding that gun in your hand, touching the barrel against your temple, tasting its metallic-ness on your tongue. You press that blade against your wrist, wishing you could cut all the way down and through the bone.

But contrary to the belief of many, self-mutilation is very different from being suicidal. There are a couple of different definitions of self-mutilation, self-injury (SI) or self-harm. One is at the beginning of this book. Another is along the lines of an intentional act of physical self-injury without the intent to die. A large number of people who SI have also attempted suicide at some point in their lives. But there is a difference between the two. Some research indicates suicide attempts stem from feelings of hopelessness, while self-mutilation comes from feelings of shame or a need to relieve tension.

There are three accepted forms of self-mutilation. The most common is referred to as "superficial self-injury." It's typically people cutting, burning, hitting, pulling out their own hair or breaking their own bones. The second type is called "stereotypical self-mutilation." This is when a person bangs her head, pushes on her eyeballs and bites herself. The third and most severe type is called "major self-mutilation." It is rare, but this is when the person may amputate limbs or do other things to permanently disfigure her body.

All three of those things could lead to accidental suicide. It's never really the intention.

I take several pills for depression, allergies, acid reflux and frequent headaches. Every Sunday, I refill my daily pill case. Sometimes I dump all the pills out into one big pile and sift through them, hold them in my hands until they are overflowing. I imagine taking them all, wondering what it would do to me, how long it would take to kill me. Or make me really, really sick. I think about all the power those pills have together. I love the feel of them in my hands and the power I have to take them or not take them.

In the end, of course, not taking them always wins out. For a while, I wondered if that meant I was strong or I was weak. To someone struggling with thoughts of suicide, to not go through with it, to not be strong enough to take one's own life, is a sign of weakness.

But to "normal" people, suicide is just the easy way out. It's not being strong enough to get a grip and take on life. With life being the thing that really takes the strength, not suicide.

The same can go for cutting. Does slicing through your own skin make you strong or make you weak? That's actually a loaded question that can have a lot of different interpretations.

Being strong by cutting makes you weak overall. It makes you dependant and addicted. It can actually make you more sensitive, more prone to flying off the deep end with little provocation. Because you're strong about it makes you weak against using it. It's so easy to turn to that you become weak in your own strengths.

Cutting can be used to stop feeling or start feeling.

Sometimes, a cutter, such as myself, feels everything. Every single emotion slams into her at 100 miles per hour. But those emotions don't go out the backdoor. They hit full speed into the spine, then shatter into a million pieces. They overtake her body, mind and soul until there is no room inside of her for anything else. Those shards of emotions jab and stick and slice her insides, and it all hurts so badly. Much more than anyone can imagine. Cutting brings it all into focus, gives her one thing to concentrate on, instead of those hundreds of pieces. Focusing on the blade, cutting the skin, the bit of pain, the blood, brings her down, brings her back to reality. And in her head, it's the emotional release she's been looking for, the release she's been needing. The emotions flow out, mixed with the blood. And, once again, she feels calm. She feels nothing—what she's wanted all along.

Then, on the other end of the spectrum, feeling nothing becomes scary. Some self-mutilators don't feel anything at all. They walk around feeling completely numb. Feeling is human, after all. So, if she has no feelings, is she human? She's breathing, but is she alive? She's bleeding, but is she alive?

Cutting is a way to inflict pain—a simple, human emotion. Once she feels that, she can breath a sigh of relief because she's feeling, even if she's feeling pain. She is, in fact, alive and human now that she's cut herself.

The following is an excerpt from a story I once wrote, but whose ending is still unknown:

"That night I dream of falling in a pond…falling down too far to swim back up. I look up, can see leaves falling over the water, covering me so no one could see me even if they were looking. I don't reach up for those leaves, don't reach for any help at all. I feel calm. I look at my hands through the water in front of me. They look wavy, like the water. They are nearly transparent. I think I can actually see water running through my veins.

If there's water, then there's no blood…no blood to make me human like everyone else still on the other side of the leaves.

What if it's still in there and I just can't see it because the water is hiding it? If I bled it all out, under water, the faster I can stay here forever—covered safely, floating, weightless….

I need to bleed, need to see my own blood coming out of my own skin…draining all the things inside me; the things I hate and the things that make me who I am. I put it in my mouth and bite down. Through the skin.

When I taste the blood, I bite down even harder to make it come faster…

Please please…God just take me….please…."

July 16

I feel so empty today. Like there's nothing in me. No heart (except I know it's there because it's broken, and it hurts), no soul, no breath.

I feel like that book title, "She's Come Undone."

The only thing that has kept me going so far, and I guess keeps me hanging on by a very thin thread is my music.

It's strange how I seem to have a direction for my life, but I don't have a desire for life. I guess. I'm not sure.

If anything can keep me going, it's the desire…actually, the need…to succeed.

If I make it through alive, I will. In that respect. Then I'll succeed in everything else, I hope.

How would/should I do it? When should I do it? I will kill myself. I will enjoy every minute.

July 20

I wish this cut were deeper.

Like, to the vein.

August 28

This book, *Saving the Lives of Adolescent Girls* is pretty interesting. I find myself comparing myself as a teenager to these girls I'm reading about.

Reading through this stuff really makes me want to examine myself…from when I was a teenager to now.

Sometimes I think that these girls are like am I now…depressed, uncertain, self-deprecating and capable of self-harm.

I don't like the idea that I'm acting like a teenage girl. I'm 22 now…I shouldn't be able to compare me now to 15, 16 and 17-year-olds.

I don't know if that idea scares me more than it makes me sick.

This psychiatrist/psychologist really encourages her patients to write. I feel I'm very lucky that I already had that all my life. I've always known writing and music were my ways out…my positive ways of dealing with stuff.

I don't know how I feel about getting some help. I guess it could work to help me understand myself and feel better about myself. But then I'd have to have somebody who doesn't know or love me judge me after I tell her every bad thing about myself. It's hard enough admitting that sort of thing to myself…let alone somebody I don't even know.

I could probably write a novel based solely on myself. Although I don't think it would make much sense.

This [journal] has been pretty damn positive so far. I almost hate to ruin it with all this talk and psychological cogitating. But it's on my mind…and writing is the key.

I have to admit, that was pretty cool what happened with that knife this morning.

In that book I'm reading, the doctor always has the girls write down or record positive thoughts about themselves or when things make them happy or pleased.

I did do that for a few days. Maybe I didn't try hard enough or maybe I gave up because nothing was positive about myself.

I think I have a lot of trouble being comfortable with material things. I mean, I have a ton of them…but when I stop and look around, realize how much I have, I get so embarrassed.

Or when I decide I'd like some ice cream and have to go buy it…or when kids are deliberating over what kind of snack thing they want…I get such a funny feeling. Like who are we to be upset there's only chocolate and vanilla ice cream, no twist. Who are we to have a grab-bag [party] and get excited over fish boxer shorts.

Who am I to get a new computer…drive a car…eat a popsicle.

Thinking about it seriously makes me sick.

I think I'm having an anxiety attack right now. Wow.

Reason I don't swallow all the pills in the house—I have trouble taking pills, and I would rather die any other way than asphyxiating myself on pills.

August 29
Skin is tough. I need a sharper knife.

I think I do appreciate what's good in my life. I do. I just don't appreciate the good I bring into my own life. Or anyone else's.

October 5
Oh, my God. I think I have a personality disorder. For real. A borderline personality.

***

It's interesting, the professional opinions of counselors, therapists, doctors. I read *Girl, Interrupted* by Susanna Kaysen for a college class once. It's about a girl with a borderline personality. I could see a lot of me in her and her in me. That didn't frighten me or make me nervous. It did make me wonder if I needed to be hospitalized like her, even though I'm not convinced the things she was given during her stay were what she really needed.

For a long time after I finished reading it, I considered the book. I carried around a secret with me at all times. The secret was I was sick with a borderline personality—I had self-diagnosed myself based on the book. I spent a lot of time thinking about it and wondering about it. Borderline personality...did I really have a "title?" Especially one with a negative connotation? But if I did have a title, maybe I could get some kind of treatment or help or whatever I needed so I could feel better. Isn't that what titles were for?

I had a counselor who later reiterated the fact that I was, indeed, borderline. I never really got a good explanation of it, though. Never fully understood what was wrong with me or how to fix it. I felt relieved, though. Someone else was backing up my theories about myself. Finally, someone knew about me and could help me.

Later on, after that person told me I was beyond her help, my new therapist told me she didn't think I was borderline at all. Even if I was, "so what?" Everything I'd depended on went spinning. For all that time, I'd classified myself, thinking that was all I needed to get "better." Now, Dr. Deb was telling me titles and classifications meant nothing. She said that it was an empty thing to be categorized. She said there wasn't any difference in how she would handle me.

I suppose, of course, there is a big difference between telling someone they are borderline and say, schizophrenic. But it was strange to be told I wasn't something when I thought I was for so long.

Who knows what another doctor might tell me. He or she might put a lot of emphasis on titles and confuse me even more. It's interesting to hear professionals talk about who should be called what and how someone should be treated.

It's interesting to hear regular people talk about mental problems, as well. As if they have any clue, unless they have a few themselves. They throw words like "schizo" and "psychotic" around like any person having a normal meltdown could possibly become "crazy" in a matter of five minutes. I'm guilty of that too, but at least I have some qualification in the matter.

Remember, I've been all of those things myself, and more.

There is always someone who still thinks getting help, turning to someone trained to deal with certain life issues, is a bad thing. Still says "shrink" like it's the word "fuck" or something. Mental illness really isn't a joke because it's so real to so many people. For some of those people, it can be agonizing.

People joke with each other about getting put on Prozac or whatever—me included. But don't forget that for a lot of people, those drugs mean the difference between life and death; they really work. Same goes for counseling. Some may insist it's all a racket and all doctors are quacks. Some are, some aren't. But the doctors and meds are a big part of life for a big chunk of the population.

October 28
I think this cutting thing is like doing anything. It takes practice. Practice to get better and stronger.

***

It's practically a documented fact that cutting is a drug. In fact, it *is* documented that cutting releases endorphins throughout the body; The same endorphins that course through a person's blood stream while exercising or having sex. Endorphins are pain-killing substances in the body released by stress or trauma. In other words, they stimulate the body and that feels good, just another reason the cutter wants it and needs it.

The more someone uses it, the more she ends up wanting and needing it. The more she uses it, the more she has to do it to get the same effect, just like drugs. The more she does it, the more dangerous it becomes. She cuts more, in more places—she makes the cuts longer and deeper, gets more used to the sight of the blood dripping out of her, doesn't feel as much when she cuts.

She can't see past the blade of that razor to a future without it.

November 9
I am so sensitive today. For real. Crying so hard because I didn't make a salad [for dinner].

I think that if I tried my hardest, I would still think I didn't try enough.

And I have enough guilt in this world for every person in it.

For real. Feeling so bad for the guy at the bar because he had no one to sing to? That was the worst. I'm still hurting over it.

And when I turned [a boyfriend] down to go back later on? Man. It was just a bad day all around.

[A friend] says she does so much for other people. She has no idea what it's like to have so much guilt inside you…she has no idea what it's like to put yourself on the line for another person.

December 18

How do people ever get over the things they have done in their lives? Does everyone obsess over that behind closed doors as I do? Or do people really forget about those things and not care? How could that be possible? Would I want to be like that? Would I want to be careless and ...I can't think of the word.

I'm not sure. If it would free me of all the guilt I carry, maybe.

But maybe this guilt drives me along this world. Maybe it's what makes me always want to put other people first. What makes me try to be the best....

I don't know if that's a good way to be. But I don't know any other way to be. So, I don't know if it's a bad way to be.

I don't know if I feel too much...[A friend] says I'm passionate. So far, this doesn't seem to be working in my favor.

<shakes head> This is terrible.

I don't know if everything I need to improve on is just stuff for myself—like how I feel about myself and treat myself.

But I've said before, I'm not sure I want to change any of that. Because it's who I am now. And what keeps me going.

***

I have to think guilt is something we all struggle with. Some, like me, struggle with it more than others, say like a mass-murderer.

It's always played a huge roll in my life and my coping techniques, though I'm not sure I could ever find out why. I've just naturally always felt bad about things or responsible for things that weren't really my fault, or little things I shouldn't have even thought twice about; normal, daily mishaps, that sort of thing. I would do all sorts of things I didn't really want to do because I felt guilty. And when I did say no to something, I was plagued by guilt for days. Sometimes I would cry about it. Sometimes I would get depressed about it. And much of the time, I'd cut over it, feeling it an appropriate punishment for not doing what I felt I should have done, even if I didn't want to. Or even if it was no big deal. To me, anything and everything was a big deal. I was oversensitive and overreacted to a lot of things. I would constantly apologize for no reason. I would nearly beat people over the head with apologies if I thought I wronged them. No one would ever admit to the things I thought I'd done or shown through my actions. Since they didn't, I figured I must be right and they are just being polite by not saying anything.

Anything would set me off; from a weird look someone gave me, to a flippant comment from someone to feeling like I didn't do something well enough.

That became a major problem when I got into the media business because perfection is a must. I'd always strived for it, but could never quite reach it, anyway. And it was completely unobtainable when I got my first jobs in my major.

It's a fast-paced field no matter in what city one starts. Mine was in Pittsburgh; as a news writer for a top 20 television station, with no-nonsense producers and reporters, a not-very-user-friendly computer system and a huge set of rules and deadlines. I was very hard on myself if producers changed scripts I wrote, (which will happen until the day I quit this business or die, whichever comes first) or I couldn't keep up with the number of scripts assigned to me. I got very upset when an anchor read my scripts and was critical of them, or made fun of them. Working a number of different shifts with different producers messed with me too, because I had a hard time keeping track of which producer wanted what written and how. I worked there for six months, in which time I did learn how to manage time and handle situations. I did improve and did make friends. Unfortunately, my coping with the stresses didn't get any healthier.

Nor did they when I took a job at a central Pennsylvania station as an on-air reporter. It was a whole new world; a new home, a new job and a whole new set of responsibilities. I was a bureau reporter and what they call a "one-man band," meaning I reported and shot my own video....lugged around damn near 75 pounds of equipment in high heels and skirts, while setting up and covering stories in one county the same as any reporter would do with the help of someone else. It was a lot of pressure, especially for the first year when I was trying so hard to find a place in the company and find myself. Nothing was ever good enough for me—not my voice, my clothes, my face, my writing, my shooting, my on-air presence or dealing with other people in and out of the office.

I felt completely alone, isolated in a place where I didn't know anyone. I didn't have any friends. I missed my mom and my life in Pittsburgh. I couldn't seem to get in the groove of finding stories to do each day.

My feelings, inadequacies and the guilt over not being good enough got the better of me. So, I cut all the time. In my bathroom, on my bed, in the shower, which was my favorite spot to cut. I did it while I was driving in the work van to and from stories, to and from the station. I cut in the bathroom at work. I would uncurl paperclips and jab the ends into my skin underneath my desk. Staples worked too.

I had an endless supply of band-aids in the van and in my workbag.

My coping technique was never far because I couldn't be without it. That was a sense of security because I knew the razors or knives or paperclips were right there with me whenever I needed them.

It turned out to be a false sense of security, of course. It was what it took to get me through each day. Ironically, each day I made it through by cutting felt like a big achievement to me.

Looking back, I know that I should not have had to feel that way; it should have been the opposite.

MARISSA CARNEY

Ode to Bedford

Working in Bedford sure opens your eyes,
To the world of agriculture and an interesting variety of guys.
Finding a lead story is only wishful thinking,
You're lucky to get a few that are ever worth "skylinking."
Going live at noon, five and six are as crazy thoughts, we know,
As ending Springs Hotel stories and finding who put Notestein 6
feet below.
It's sad when the commissioners are your three best friends,
And stories about cows, hunting and the economy never end.
Frustration is an emotion we very often know;
Like carrying 800 pounds of equipment in the heat, rain and snow.
Never beating the paper and days with nothing to do,
Hours of drive time and people who won't interview.
Waiting for hours at Central Court...what a mess!
But considering the county, we would expect no less.
Feeling out of the station loop, communicating only by phone,
Too many hungry men-dogs in Bedford, and feeling like a bone.
But through the job's ups and downs,
There's lots of growing in leaps and bounds.
A great first or second job to mold our style,
Experience and a few people that make it worthwhile.
Ode to "Befford" and all who've reported from it,
We hold our heads high, 'cuz it's really not shit.

MRC 2001

My therapist once asked me to make a list of all the things I felt guilty about. It was easy to start, not so easy to stop. I had so many things that I just quit putting them down because I figured one page was enough at once. Looking back over them now, they still make sense to me, and I can still relate to and feel them inside of me. I guess there are things you just always carry around with you, no matter how you try to forget them or store them in your head. However, I feel that they have become just that; a part of me. Not me. More like the veins I see running zig-zag through the palm of my left hand. They are there, but only if I really bother to look, to notice them.

Marissa's List of Guilt
I feel guilty...

1. That I feel guilty
2. That I have all of the things I do
3. Because I *am* happy
4. That I don't try harder with my father because maybe he has changed
5. That I don't try harder with [my sisters] by visiting more
6. Because I don't think [my sisters] are the best things to ever happen to me
7. Because my mother isn't as happy as she could be
8. That my mother and brother have been hurt as much as they have by my father
9. Because I've hurt them too
10. Because I make my mother cry
11. That my mother worries about me as much as she does
12. That I don't talk about certain things with my mother. I know she wants me to, and we are close, but I just can't
13. That sometimes I don't put my all into my job
14. Because I am so sensitive and apparently take things out of context
15. Because I feel misunderstood
16. Because I don't care as much about my old friends and keeping

them happy anymore

17. That I feel really spiritual and close to God, but I never know if it's enough
18. That I don't like to go out and drink and party
19. That I'm not a very social person
20. That I put my friends through so much when I was cutting
21. That I cut right in front of Trisha and Jesse that night in Virginia
22. Because of everything we all had to go through afterward
23. That my mother had to see the stitches on my wrist
24. That I'm not traditional in my romantic relationships
25. That I make more money than my mother
26. Because I'm tired all of the time
27. That I get irritated with my managers and let them know that
28. That I'm not a better person
29. That I broke a lot of hearts
30. Because I'm so often critical of others
31. Because I'm not sure I give people enough attention that they want
32. Because my brother and I were a burden on my mother
33. I feel guilty for other things, but I don't even know what they are; the guilty feeling is just there, almost all of the time

December 31

And I'm right back to where I've been for so long.

The dark. A place of loneliness, depression and anger. That dark place that turns red with my blood.

I don't understand.

Something just might get out of hand, and I could be gone.

And why do I write that like I give a shit. I don't care. I don't give a shit if I live or die.

If Heaven is such a great place, who cares about life here on earth?

How can I when all I feel is pain and hurt and tears on my cheeks. When the only thing that brings me happiness is music.

Music can't last forever. Well, maybe it could, but music can't fill every void I have forever.

I can't keep doing this, hiding how I feel and pretending to be happy for everyone else's sake.

Why do I keep getting screwed like this? I feel like I'm always getting fucked by my heart.

January 3, 2001
And so it goes.
Once again I gave it all and
My heart pays the price.
I know that it isn't broken, but
There wasn't much left to break
Anyway.
And now I've come full circle to where
I've been all along.
Flat on my back, no breath at all,
Surrounded by those shards of my heart
That cut my skin deeper every time I
Fall.

January 4
Where is the light? My light at the end of this tunnel. I don't think I ever got out of it. There are just, like, windows, sort of teases, inside it.

But I pass them by trying to find my way out—to that permanent light.

Does anyone who isn't dead really have a permanent light? Or do they feel enclosed in this tunnel like I do?

I don't know.

February 12
So many kids or adults who grew up without a father always say something about feeling guilty that the father left.

I have no idea if I feel that way. Do I feel guilty…like it's my fault? I really don't think so.

However, I carry a lot of guilt around because of how much my mom had to go through…and how hard it was for her and all the things she had to give up to get [my brother] and I through school.…It just really hurts me in that respect.

So many girls without dads go out and get pregnant and all that…I kind of think that it must not have affected me that much if I turned out to be so normal.

And I do think…for the most part…I'm pretty normal.

I think the term "daddy" should be used only for fathers who are around and love their kids and all that. Too many people just call a father "Daddy" just because…Like, "my baby's daddy," or something like that. It drives me nuts.

Baby Sister

My dreams are now yours to carry
I probably don't want them
anyway.
Fairytale endings are better suited for you.

You can pick up where my hopes have left off
and give rise to my broken family.
Your shoulders should be free.

We share the same blood,
but now my burdens are your wings.

Baby sister,
I hope you fly

10/31/04 – 11/3/04

I could write a whole separate book about fathers and growing up without one. The older I get, the more I think about it. It used to not bother me that my father left. In fact, I wanted him to and was glad when he did. I couldn't stand him anymore, anything about him; the way he treated my mom, his selfishness, his teeth and spit cans, his homework lying around, his saxophone playing....

My dad worked in the coal mines when I was little. Then, when I was 12 or so, he decided to go back to school to be an occupational therapist. This was going to help the family because he wouldn't have shift work, he'd be making more money and we wouldn't be so poor anymore. I remember that we all thought it was a good idea and were even excited about it.

So, he started up classes at a college about 45 minutes or so from our home.

It's hard for me to separate things by year; what happened when and how it all went down. I just have certain memories of things up until he didn't come back when I was maybe in 9th grade. And the divorce was final as I finished up my sophomore year of high school.

I don't know when I really started noticing the changes around the house and with my father, but I know that I started becoming friends with depression by the time I was 13 over it all. It's funny to me now, actually. How could I have been depressed when I was the one lobbying so hard for him to leave? But I know it's true. I used to have this notebook that I'd trade back and forth with a friend of mine at the time. It was sort of one big, ongoing note. I'd have it one night, she'd have it the next. Her entries were always happy, full of teenage funnies and joys. Mine were full of dropped hints about my home life and how sad I was. I would end most of my entries with something like, "I'm so depressed. Sigh...." But I never got much of a response from my friends. I guess being that age, not many of them knew how to handle my situation or the way I was feeling. That isolated me even more, I think. I was hurt, confused and my support system at the time couldn't understand.

I know there are millions of kids out there who grew up like me and were going through the same things I did. I'm not trying to make my story any worse than anyone else's. I'm just relaying it because it really does a play a part in my life, no matter how much I once tried to deny it.

I do know the challenges and stresses that come with getting a degree. I know there must have been a lot of pressure on my dad to succeed and keep a family at the same time. But I know it can be done. I still don't think there was any reason for the things he did to us as a whole and separately during those years.

He didn't have a job at the time. I don't think my mom or my brother or I required much of him, except that he be around once in a while, that he talk to us, eat dinner with us, be a husband and father, still.

My mother once explained to me that much of what happened was because my father didn't go to college before. She said she thought he felt like he missed out on the college life; the atmosphere, the friends, the parties, the women. She felt that's what led to the change in his personality. Which may be, but I'm still not convinced it's an excuse.

I guess it's all the little things I remember that led up to me wanting my father to leave. Once he did, all the little things that happened after that kept me happy that he was gone.

I remember things like my brother finding a box of condoms hidden in the basement wall paneling under my father's "desk." Not that I knew much about condoms at that point, but I knew they wouldn't be hidden in a wall. I also knew that my dad shouldn't really need them with my mother since he'd had a vasectomy.

I remember my brother telling me that he listened in on a phone conversation between my dad and some other woman as they exchanged sappy "I love you's."

I remember him staying out until 10 or 11 at night at his "saxophone lessons," and him suddenly wearing a saxophone charm around his neck, given to him by a "friend."

I remember him leaving me at home one night, walking over to my grandparents' house, taking one of their cars without their permission and going to some beer party.

I remember not being allowed to go into the basement and play with my toys because he was down there "studying."

One of the most heartbreaking memories was my brother's 18th birthday. My mother always made us whatever we wanted for dinner on our birthdays. That year, my brother only wanted cereal—that's it.

My mom tried to dress it up a little by buying several boxes of cereal (the good stuff we normally couldn't afford) and setting boxes on each side of his bowl place setting. My brother refused to eat until my father got home from classes, though. Dad picked that day to be about two hours late getting home. I forget what his excuse was, but I know I didn't buy it. I know there really isn't any excuse for being late on your child's 18th birthday dinner, when you know the whole family is waiting for you.

I remember sitting there, seeing the hurt in my brother's eyes as we waited. The pain and frustration in my mother's as she tried to coax him to start eating because we all had places to be after dinner. I know she was hurting because her son was. I know she was pissed at my father. I just sat there, feeling uncomfortable and wishing I could take both of their pain away.

It was worse when Dad came home. The tension got even thicker since Mom was mad, my brother was still upset and Dad thought nothing was wrong at all.

Another memory that still makes me sad is the time I was up getting ready for school and my dad was walking out the door to get to his classes. Mom was standing at the door in her nightgown saying goodbye. When Dad started to leave, she asked him, "Can I get a kiss?" My father turned around to look at her and just smiled. It's hard to explain, I guess, but the smile and his body language clearly stated he didn't want to kiss his wife goodbye. He stalled for several seconds, then leaned over to peck her. Mom closed the door after him with tears in her eyes, and I felt like dying.

To make a saga short, all of this went on until my dad left for an internship in Florida (why he picked such a faraway state when he had a family in Pennsylvania, we can only surmise he was trying to get away from us) and he never came home again.

In my blurry memory, I'm not even sure I knew where he was for a year or so because we didn't hear from him. I was in junior high school at the time and was just trying to make it through day after day at that hell hole, without having to think and wonder about him too.

I know I visited him once, later on, when he lived in New Jersey, after the separation was official, during the divorce. He took me and a friend to New York to see a show. When he dropped us off to my mother at our designated meeting point, I started crying pretty hard. I didn't understand it. Why was I crying over someone I didn't even know or like? I suppose it was just confusion over the whole thing.

I didn't see him much after that for several years. Didn't hear from him all that often either. He missed most of the holidays and forgot a few birthdays. He missed dance recitals, school musicals, band events, parades, softball games, victories, hurts…he missed me growing up.

He remarried and then later, he and his new wife had a daughter. Ten days before my 24th birthday. Then they had another little girl, who came along just about two years later; a few weeks after I turned 26.

Talking to him or seeing him can still be so uncomfortable, frustrating, sad and just about any other emotion anyone can feel at once in a situation like that.

I guess things started getting harder for me as I got older and older and really began to realize what he had done to our family and to me. We were ditched, dropped, abandoned. When you really start to think about something like that, it's easy to take it hard.

Feeling that I was ditched by my father meant I wasn't good enough, what I always thought in my heart anyway.

What's hard now is letting those feelings go—inadequacy, anger for what he put us all through, anger that he got away with it and simply started a brand new life without considering us. It's hard to just let go and move on, valuing the relationship with my sisters, but leaving him out of it.

I guess most of the time I feel so caught that I don't think about it at all, just kind of go with the flow. Even now, he still has some kind of hold on me, some kind of power. I still talk to him when he calls me on the phone. I still act comfortable around him whenever he's visiting or I'm visiting. In the back of my mind, I know that I still have a father. I still remember all the fun, happy, good times. I still feel like I should honor that, forget my own bitter and resentful feelings and make sure he feels that I'm okay with how things played out. That I'm okay with everything he's done. Like I should just adjust and deal with it, move on. If only it were that easy for me. Sometimes, I know that I long to be a part of his life and he mine. But most of the time, I'm fine without him, thinking it's him who's missing out on everything good.

There is the argument that kids need both parents in the household. Being from a single-parent home, and being all grown up now, I can see both points of view, though I don't totally think that either one is correct.

One parent who loves you with all of his or her heart is better than two parents who don't love you at all. Two parents who love you with all their hearts but don't live together are better than parents who do and don't pay any attention. Children need love, and plenty of it. But getting it from only one parent does not make all of those kids delinquents with drug problems with seven children out of wedlock. It doesn't make them all criminals with mental problems. Anyone can be a criminal with mental problems. My mother has always said it would have been a lot easier to raise me and my brother with a spouse. I have no doubt about that. I also have no doubt it can be a lot nicer for children to have both parents. But they can still grow up to be normal, loving, kind and all those good things being raised just by their mother or father.

I think I have. I admitted earlier the circumstances surrounding my one-parent home *may have* contributed to my disorder. But it certainly wasn't the only thing that did. I don't believe that for a minute.

My mom remarried when I was 18, the summer before I started college. I could write a whole novel about that too, but I won't. It's interesting to compare my experience with that of other blended families. Getting another parental figure so late in life, after I'd been alone with Mom for so long was an experience, to say the least. I look back and wonder how families do it. How do they make it work, even if it's not going all that well.

It was a tough adjustment for all of us, I do know that.

A lot of things changed just for me. Things weren't as relaxed and open as they used to be. I began to feel like a stranger in my own home. I began to feel like I didn't matter and like my feelings weren't important anymore

I know that's a typical reaction to someone new in the house that most kids feel, yet it seems different.

It was hard to watch Mom struggle through with her second marriage. Hard to balance my feelings out about it all. For all the times I was mad and upset and cried and stalked out of the house, slamming the door behind me, there were the times that everything was really great.

I often ask myself what I'd be like had my parents stayed together—had I grown up a coal miner's daughter forever, with no steps or halfs. It's a question I just can't answer, though. Or even begin to speculate on. In fact, when I start asking myself those kinds of questions, I don't think about them for too long. I hate to think of myself as a different person because I spent too much time wishing I were. I don't like to think of the things I could have done differently under different circumstances. I don't always like the direction my life went, but I do like knowing how I turned it all around, how I used it all to create something that can help others. When I don't dwell on things, I like the person I have become through all of this. I like the good things I do for other people, the way I make them laugh and smile and appreciate themselves.

Now, I'm not saying it was easy for Mom, me or my brother. Hell, no. Mom was exhausted, my brother spiraling downward to a perpetual state of confusion and loneliness, me...Well, I'm not exactly sure. I don't know how Mom or my brother would describe me during those first few years we were on our own. Was I the clown, trying to keep things light and smiley? Was I the dark one? The one who acted out? Did it not matter at all because everyone was too into their own grief and pain?

I felt alone a lot. Helpless a lot.

Mom hid in her room a lot, and I could hear her crying a lot.

I could never quite bring myself to knock on her door; it wouldn't be closed if I were welcome inside. I missed my mom during those times, and I hated that she was hurting. The worst of those nights was one Christmas night, probably the first after my father was gone. The day had been all right, but around 8:00 p.m., Mom disappeared. She went into her room and didn't come out the rest of the night. I don't remember her even saying goodnight or Merry Christmas or I love you. My lip still trembles when I think of that night. I stood outside her door for a while, shifting back and forth on my feet, wondering if I should knock or just leave her alone. I finally went to my own room, closed the door and put a Christmas CD on. I must have listened to "Oh, Holy Night" about a million times as I stared out my window at what I imagined was the star of Bethlehem. Even though I tried to think of the magic of Christmas and that star, my sadness could not, would not, be quenched.

But still, the human spirit and heart go on. For as many sad, depressing things my family and I went through, the good memories during those times are there, too—strong and vibrant; watching Mom in the mirror get ready for something, cleaning the house with her on Wednesdays while Taylor Dane or Tony Tone Toni! blasted in the background, disco-dancing in the living room to Taste of Honey's "Boogie Oogie Oogie," taking road trips to Ohio to visit family, watching our favorite TV shows, eating ice cream right out the carton or just sitting near each other quietly reading while she paid the bills.

My brother and I trying to make the perfect bowl of cream of wheat, daring each other to run barefoot through the snow from our yard to our grandparents' yard, tag-team wresting in the basement or having a ping-pong tournament, watching reruns of the old *Saturday Night Live*, me doing his homework for him…the list goes on and on.

What I know for sure, without any confusion, is that through all of that, good or bad, my mother was there. My mother—my strength in just about everything I do—my single-parent mother who gave me all the love I ever needed.

***

August 15
What a sucky-ass day. I fear tomorrow will be just as bad, if not worse. I have no ideas…well, I have one, but it will never work out probably. I need that one dude from PennDOT, but I'll never get back before his meetings.

God, I'm so unhappy. I didn't want to have to admit that. But I have to.

Where do I go from here…what do I do? How do I get happy again? Can I? With all this stuff, can I get back to me again? I have no idea.

April 4, 2002
Oh, God. That was a bad one. I need to bring a razor here to work. I was going nuts and had to use a paper clip.

I don't know what brought that on.

April 9
So, the more I think about it…the more I wonder if starting therapy would help. I'm sure I've written about this before…but everyone seems to think I need it so bad.

I wonder if the person could tell me if I'm obsessive/compulsive. Or help me stop feeling guilty all the time. Or understand why I'm so jealous and sensitive…

Even if all that is possible…would it really help me? I hate needing help.

April 11
Anyway, I came to work today and Kellie said she had something

for me. It tturned out to be info on counselors and whatnot…she said Trisha gave it to her to give to me in case she wasn't here. Somehow, they ending up talking about it all?

Kellie said they both knew about it and talked about it…interesting. I'd love to know what was said. I think I'll call Trisha tonight.

Kellie said if I didn't call first, they were going to call for me…

I've never had anyone take this so seriously…not even myself. It's weird…but nice in a way.

I just don't know…can I really do this? Do I really want to give it up?

Like my poem says—I'm afraid to be without it. It really has become a part of me.

I don't know what else to do without it.

Some days, I'm sure I want to go as far as I can…but not because I want it to be the end—just because that's how I feel…depending on my mood—how bad things are or how bad I feel….

How do I get this "person" to understand? Understand it all, understand I don't want to give it up?

I've made such a mess of this. I should go…and be done with it.

Hear what the doc has to say, tell them I went and be done with it.

This whole thing is just ridiculous. I think I like the fact that they worry and want to help…it's nice to know people really care.

The look sometimes in Kellie's eyes…I'm, like, worth helping in them.

I'm not sure if I meant to scare either of them—I don't think so. I hate to think I did, though.

I'm trying to put myself in their shoes, and I'm not sure how I'd feel or what I'd do.

Maybe I don't bring it up anymore? But they, or Kellie, at least, is pretty persistent. I don't know.

April 14
I have a baby sister. I have a sister.

Wow. I have so many emotions that I can't even right them—I

don't really even know them.

A sister. Wow.

<Later the same day>

I have a sister.

April 22

I'm on hold on right now with the [counseling program].

Not anymore now, but I was. How strange…it's so weird to answer these questions. There's no holds barred—there can't be. But answering those simple questions made me so shy…I can hardly imagine how I'll be able to talk, to someone face to face.

The first lady was really nice—patient and caring, making sure I was ok and safe at the time.

The second lady was all right—she made me shy, though. Not sure why…

The lady said, from what I told her, it seems I don't know why I do what I do, that what I do is pretty severe way of dealing with stuff. She said some do it to actually feel something or else they'll be numb and others do it out of depression. I know it's not because I'm numb…I am pretty sure the feeling is a reason why.

She says she thinks I know it's not good because I hide it from others, and I if I really thought it was okay, I wouldn't hide it at all. Interesting—never thought of that before. It's probably true. Or maybe I hide it because I think it's okay, but others won't…?

The next big step is to actually find someone to talk to….how embarrassing.

The whole thing is just so strange.

Why am I never good enough?

April 23

Happy birthday to me!

Counseling might not work out for me. We only have a co-pay of 50 %, and that is *after* I reach a $200 deductible. I think that's crap.

In this business, there should be better help for mental health. And that's a fact.

***

These last few years of my life, as I write this, things started to go downhill for me. I really started to crack up. I never slept. I came a breath away from being 302'ed into a mental hospital....twice. I had surgery on my throat and was put on medication for it. I developed allergies and mild asthma. I learned how to cry and so it seemed like I did it all of the time. I cut myself so badly that I needed stitches and got put on an anti-depressant.

That seems like a lot for a year and a half.

I do believe wisdom comes with age, and since I aged about 20 years after the Hospital Night, I must have gotten *a lot* wiser. I feel wiser.

I like to think I'm the kind of person who doesn't take a lot of things for granted. But in the last few years, I began to appreciate everything in a whole new, fresh way. Simple things. Watching the rain through a window, the sound of wind through trees, a pretty sunset, my own breathing.

I've always been a pretty physical person, craving hugs and kind words from family and friends. And then I started probably going a little overboard with it all. At least some of my friends may say that. I started writing letters and notes all the time, telling my friends how much I loved them and appreciated them. I bought them little gifts and constantly tried to touch them somehow, through hugs or just by patting their backs or something. The philosophy being I shouldn't be ashamed to let people know they are loved. If something should happen to me, I don't want to be dead not having told someone I loved them within the last few days.

It makes perfect sense to me. I recently re-read *Tuesdays with Morrie*, one of my favorite books of all time. I totally related to Morrie and his obsession, really, with human contact. I loved how he wasn't embarrassed by it either. I especially loved how those who came in contact with him began to see its importance.

I only wish everyone could.

I began to enjoy life a little more. I learned how to say no to people and do more for myself. I started down the long road of feeling less guilty about everything in life. I started to let things go and take baby steps forward in my life, weeding out what's important and what's not. It was a small taste of true freedom. I loved it. Perhaps I finally let my guard down and that's why I started falling apart—but things fall apart. Sometimes they need to break up completely before the glue to put it all back together can start sticking.

April 24

I've come to the conclusion that no one...well now see? I have to revise that statement. It's hard to come by people who can be the kind of friend they should be. If that makes sense.

Nobody really ever wants to hear others talk about themselves. And nobody really ever wants to listen to someone else's problem. Yet everyone wants to talk about themselves and their problems...it's frustrating sometimes.

I don't talk all that much about things I should, really. That's because it's hard to talk about it all—and simply because nobody cares.

If I went to a real counselor and talked...I doubt he or she would care either. And they're paid to care. I don't understand people most of the time.

I guess. It doesn't really matter. I wish, though, that just once, someone would come to me first. Come and start a conversation about me with me. I would once like to really feel that someone cares about me.

Other than family. That's a given.

Am I being selfish, greedy? I don't know that it's wrong to want to feel the basic things in life...genuinely?

If so, then I guess I'm just a big, greedy bitch.

May 23

Mary...M.S N.C.C. My new friend? Not sure I can say that yet...or ever. But my new, uh, listener, I guess is a good word.

I finally decided to check out some counseling.

My first week was last week. I wasn't as nervous as I thought I would be. I was still nervous—I had no idea of what to expect or if I would like the woman or even feel as though I could talk to her...

I'm still not completely sure of how I feel about her—but I was able to tell her why I was there and some background. I liked the fact that she asked questions—although that's her job, but really...I don't usually talk unless someone asks something...unless it's my mom. Then I just babble on.

Anyway, she seems nice enough. I wish she really, like, cared about me...I don't think counselors really truly care. I didn't really want to leave, actually. I was somewhat comfortable there, and it just felt nice to have someone ask and listen to my answers.

It's weird...when I left there last week, I wondered why I waited so long get to into this.

I still have part of me that wishes I didn't "need" it...but I'm learning it's okay.

Although embarrassing sometimes because I don't necessarily think my life has been all that traumatic...I'm sure she's had many people come through with a real reason to complain about life.

I don't want her thinking I'm just a big baby...which I probably am—but again, I don't want her to have that opinion of me.

Last week she said I'm delightful. This week she said I'm stunning.

I guess she wouldn't just say that—she's all about the truth in her job. I guess I just don't take compliments well because most of the time I never believe them.

But she's nice enough, and I like her.

***

Deciding to get help from a professional is, indeed, a scary undertaking. I think my entries make it clear some of the struggles we face by making that step. But I do believe that it's such an important step.

With a counselor, once you learn how, you can talk freely, feel freely, be free. No one is judging you, they are just trying to help. I can tell my counselor whatever I want, whenever I want. I can switch topics, ramble and make no sense. I can be mean and get mad and cry, if I want to. Granted, it took me about a year to get to that point. But I often wonder, if I didn't have her to do all of that with, would I really be getting any better? She teaches me it's okay to feel. I don't have to cut to feel; feel better about myself, or feel anything at all. It's okay to hurt inside; in fact, it's the only way, because hurting yourself on the outside doesn't really take away the pain.

Counselors or psychologists aren't always right. And they aren't completely in your head, so they may say one thing when you know you really feel a different way. And that's okay.

Sometimes they make you mad. Sometimes they hurt your feelings.

Lucky for me, I had two who I know really cared about me and my well-being, so anytime I felt hurt by them or mad at something they said, I got over it. They weren't working with me only to get their money. My doctors are in the business to help. Once I figured that out, it was easier to open up and share my secrets.

Not that I am the best patient in the world, or the best talker. I went through several sessions where I probably didn't speak more than five words—that doesn't help much. Dr. Deb let me know that, by getting outwardly frustrated with me several times, begging me to grow up and talk about the things I wanted or needed to talk about.

No matter what, it all comes down to the patient—me. It comes down to tossing out pride, embarrassment, and whatever else just to get down to what's really there inside of me. Sitting in silence doesn't fix anything, and sooner or later, you start to resent the counselor for just letting you sit there…either while she talks about nothing relevant or stares at you waiting for some kind of comment or reaction.

The process works both ways; you have to be both receptive and giving if you ever want to get out of there or start feeling better.

Certainly, counseling isn't for everyone. But how can you know unless you at least try it with an open mind? The trick is to know when to get out. Nobody says you should have to stay in therapy forever. You don't want to feel stuck there, otherwise your main issues won't even matter anymore.

I'm not sure I would have made it this far if not for Mary and Dr. Deb. With cutting to begin with, people say you have to stop doing it for yourself. I admit, that's not the way it went for me when I first got serious about quitting. I wasn't doing it for myself at that time. I don't know that I was completely ready. I was sort of forced into it by being taken to the hospital. My friends were ready for it to be over. I was scared of losing them, so I began the journey. In counseling, I was afraid of disappointing Mary and Dr. Deb. So in that respect, I was forced into doing things a different way, looking at things differently and understanding things differently. Because I didn't want to let them down, I did things their way. After a while, they made sense. Not completely, but enough. I respected those women enough to try and do what they were telling me. It helps that neither of them ever gave up on me, even when Mary told me she couldn't counsel me anymore because I was out of her range of expertise. At first, I was devastated, thinking I must be really messed up if she couldn't treat me anymore. I'd grown to really trust her, even love her. Later, I came to realize she wasn't giving up on me. She was giving up on herself because she cared that much for me. If other people cared that much for me, maybe I really was worth caring about for myself.

May 31
I'm also starting to examine things in my life…things I never would have thought of before…for example…we've talked about growing up and feeling loved and being on my own—that sort of thing. I guess I always wondered about some things along that line when I got a little older.

Like, obviously, I know my mom loved me then too. But I don't remember her ever really playing with me, reading me stories or anything….I remember hugs and stuff…but I remember it only if I initiated it…I really was on my own a lot growing up—when I was young, and especially in high school. I don't know, though…I really liked that—independence and all. Freedom. I never thought it could have any effect on me now and my insecurities now. Maybe it doesn't—but it could and it makes sense.

That is one of my problems with therapy…you do start analyzing things and relating them to life and why you are the way you are, when maybe you're just that way because that's the way you are…

But relating these things really gives me a strange feeling— maybe because they really are true? But it's actually painful.

Another memory that comes along with being alone….I don't remember how old I was, (I may have written this before in another journal) when I snooped in my mom's journal and read she didn't enjoy spending time with her children. I know that's not true now…but maybe back then, I read that and that was the start of my perfectionism…because I thought I wasn't good enough for my own mother to like being with me? I don't know. Weird.

June 6

I really do think this job makes a person grow up…depending on what kind of person we're talking about.

Me—an already mature person to begin with, like I told that high school principal today—I've seen a lot of things doing this job that have made me grow as a person, and start to grasp what life really is.

Then again—I'm not sure I have since I have so much trouble accepting my own and valuing it.

But it really hits you when you think of stories like this…another high school student lost in a car wreck.

One minute driving down the road singing whatever song and then within minutes, she's gone. There are never any answers to this kind of thing.

I just have to thank God my family and friends are safe right now. At least I hope they are, pray they are, now and always.

So why do I value everyone else's life over my own? I certainly enjoy living and the things that go with it…but it's true that everyone else is more important—their thoughts and feelings and what they want and need…

It's better that way. I'm glad that's how I am.

Sometimes I really wonder what I'm doing here. I think I do have a passion for this job, but not as much as others. Is that wrong? Does that mean I don't belong here? What does that mean for my future? Do I have any hope of getting more passionate? Do I have to get that to get better?

Why can't I be perfect? Would I value my life more if I were?

When it comes down to it? This is how I see myself:

An overweight, ugly girl trying to do something she can't, who's selfish and stupid and doesn't deserve the things she's got.

Deserve. That's part of my problem. What am I worthy of? What do I really deserve?

I can't think of much.

Why do I have the life I have when so many other go through so much worse? I'm grateful, but it makes me sick sometimes.

I wouldn't be this messed up....there's no reason.

I make myself sick.

Garden of Eden

What's so beautiful on the outside
Looks like hell within.
Surrounded by evil, doubt and fear,
Fires of guilt send a soul up in smoke.

I believed the devil
When he told me I was nothing,
Opening my veins to his poisonous flow,
So much that I can't even bleed him out.

The angels see Eden,
But not the twisted roots and boiling blood
under the surface;
My garden where nothing grows.

12/9/03

June 11

I'm kind of scaring myself today—I don't know that I've ever felt this "strange."

It's like…I'm all lightheaded and dizzy, but my body is really heavy. I have no energy.

I don't feel "real." My head is full of crazy thoughts…I can't breathe properly…

I actually called Mary today, left a message for her to tell me I'm okay and I'm going to make it through the day….

It must be pretty bad when I call someone for help…I never do that.

I feel a little silly too. I don't want to depend on this woman. I could turn into "Bob," from *What About Bob*. The annoying patient.

I want to be strong. I want to do this myself. But the more I try and think about doing that…My God. I don't know if I can.

I've never felt this desperate about it all before.

To actually call my counselor from work just to hear her voice? God, what's happening to me?

I'm losing it. I had an image last night of my mind. How I want to rip it open and let all these things out of it. So, I can do this "healing" Mary keeps talking about.

I want to open my head and clear it all out, start over…

I started reading a book and a lot of what it's been so far is choosing to heal and how, yes, it's painful.

But I didn't really believe that my process would be until today. Now I know it is—it's worse than just going along like I'm fine.

Why is that? Why do we do this to ourselves?

And just what right do I have to walk around saying "I need to heal!" I can't even come up with one legitimate reason why….

My Lord…compared to a lot of other people…millions of other people? I grew up walking down a paved road of gold.

What right do I have? And what right do I have to ever, ever complain or burden my "friends" with my life?

They don't care…why should they?

I'm going crazy. I really am. I hate this.

And I'm starting to get attached to Mary...I don't want to because...well, I'm not sure why.

We can't be much else other than counselor/client. I don't think she'd let that happen—she'd say I'm trying to take care of her.

Can you really be "friends" with someone like that? Yet how can you not?

I want to ask her if she really cares about her patients...like, really cares.

For some reason, that answer makes a difference to me.

I want to hear her say she cares...and I want her to really mean it...yet, it might scare me a little.

Even though she's supposed to help me through this, I wonder if I'll still wear some sort of mask around her. Tell her only halves of a story because the rest embarrasses me or makes me look bad?

Who knows. What I do know is, today was a little frightening. And I still have to get through this damn piano lesson.

I had another vision today of being hurt.

Driving in my van, and a truck coming up behind me. I prayed he would hit me...that's not right. I'm not right.

I should put this down for a while.

But since I'm not at home to cut myself, I need to do something...

I am losing it.

June 14

This week, Mary told me that I'm beautiful. She said, "I tell people they're attractive, but you're beautiful. Beautiful smile, beautiful eyes, beautiful skin." She said it would be a tragedy for mankind if I killed myself, that I'm too young and too talented. I can't believe so many compliments came from one person in less than 3 minutes. It was really embarrassing.

She's starting to ask for details a lot more...about how I'm feeling and my emotions and such. That's hard for me. I don't express myself very well through spoken words to begin with...but then to have to do that about my feelings?!

It's rough. I should start making lists of things that she's been asking me, so I'm prepared the next time she asks me.

I got a weird feeling when she asked me to take my jacket off. I wanted her to see, but I didn't. I knew it was bad this week—and she does a pretty good job of not acting shocked by things. But I think I had her this time. Her touch was very gentle. I can't explain, but that's special.

I asked her if she really cares about her clients. She said yes without hesitation. I don't know what reason she has to lie…I can't imagine she's lying or has lied about anything.

I just like to know she does really care.

I'm all about the caring.

I showed her my newest poem "Cut Down." She likes it…said it was really good. She says I should get these published.

Cut Down

It was too late to be saved
When the blade cut my skin,
   (I was already gone).
The first time brought to the surface,
With my blood,
All the bad, all the hurt, everything I
Hate of me.
Once was not enough to get rid of it all.
Twice, three, ten times,
   (I like it too much)
Now it's a part of me,
   (I can't give it up).
Punishment for who I am, what I think and what I do.
The sound of breaking skin and I'm beyond
Saving because I'm not even scared.
Precision, blindly, fast and slow, I cut myself
   (Because I hate myself).
It's calm in my head with
Demons and Satin;
And in my hand is the way to keep them there,
Because I'm afraid to be without them.
   (I forget who I am without them).
It was too late to be saved
And it's too late to go back,
Now how far can I go,
cutting myself down to
Where I belong.
The red blood bleeding out the rest of me,
   (this is my security).

7/31/01 – 6/6/02

June 22

It's weird, though...my buddy asked about my arm. And he was no dummy about it...he didn't buy the neighbor's cat story. At the end of the day, he asked if he could jeopardize our friendship for a minute. He said if I ever needed to talk, I could call him because he really likes me and was concerned about my arm...I was uncomfortable. Like I was going to tell him anything....

It's nobody's business.

It's such a long way away until my next session with Mary. I really wish I could talk more to her, and put together a coherent sentence. I know you're supposed to talk in counseling...but sometimes I just can't. My mind is blank.

What I really wish is I could come up with stuff when she asks...like why do I hate myself. What do I hate about myself. I say "everything" and she says "give me examples" and I can't. Why? Because it's not true? No, that's not it. It is true. But how do you begin to break down "everything" into individual things?

June 28

Oh, Lord...give me strength to make it through the day...please. I want to cut up my arms, my legs....shred them.

Last night was weird—I wanted to stop, but no matter how much I wanted to, I didn't and that made me mad and I kept going because I was mad.

Then I was mad because none of the cuts were deep enough no matter how hard I pressed with the blade.

Another session with Mary...nothing too special. Actually, she rambled a lot, and I wasn't really following much of it.

I had things I wanted to say tonight, but I guess I'm still trying to find my voice with her and get comfortable with talking....

It's just that she catches me off with some of her questions. I can't think of what I want to say, so a lot of times I just say "I don't know" even though it may not be true...that's such a waste, but I don't know what else to do, I get uncomfortable.

So I spend the whole week coming up with the answers to old

questions that she doesn't ask again. It's frustrating.

But what is really frustrating are these feelings I'm trying to get in touch with...

It's really quite strange—I know they're there, somewhere. But I just can't find them, reach them. To find out what they are, why they're there, what to do with them, where to put them...how to get rid of them.

It's really weird.

I don't know if this counseling is going to help put me in touch and figure it all out...it would be nice...it's confusing.

I would love to get really angry...but I guess not at home and alone. Maybe at therapy...though that would be embarrassing...or else I'd really just like to cry...wussy as it is and though I'm not exactly sure what I have to cry about or what good it would do...maybe it would bring to the surface some of those things I just can't touch yet.

June 30

Being weak is a scary thing because once you taste it, it's sort of like an undertow. Sucks you in....at least that's what I see it as...which is why I'm so scared of it.

To Be Weak

It's not so hard
to be strong all the time;
To wear a mask of iron.
It's not so tough
To stand on two feet,
And keep a sense of balance,
While hurt is pulling
   One way
And pain is pulling
   The other.
It's not that bad
To be a soft net
For friends
As they begin their fall.
It's not so hard
To resist
Giving in
To the tears that threaten to
   Drag a
   Spirit
   Down.

The light from heaven
Sends its power;
How can it be that terrible
To be that strong?
It's not that hard
And I don't mind
This mask I have to wear;
  But once,
To shed my steel barrier
And expose my satin heart,
Could not be that bad,
  Once,
  Just to be weak.

July 1

Like I told Amy—I'm not sure, deep down, I've never really been happy…but when I'm dancing in any form, especially like today, I know complete happiness.

I'm so alive. Free. It's awesome.

If I didn't have writing or dancing, I would have killed myself long ago. I think I've written this before, but it's just so true. So, I guess I'm lucky in that respect…I've always had them. No wonder suicidal people who don't write kill themselves.

But when you think about it—what good is it? Just writing. It means, for me, I don't have to burden anyone else, really. I mean, it's not the same as having someone to hold onto or hear a gentle voice…

Now that I think about it…you really miss out on that…when you just use a journal.

But it must be damn helpful because I'm still alive.

Isn't it funny—there are so many people out there in the world…a lot of jerks, but probably just as many really cool, nice people.

It's sort of sad to think I'll never meet them. Like there are little, tiny holes in my life where strangers I would get along with and grow to love should be.

Weird.

Crazy things happen in life—I have some of them documented in these pages. For what, I'm not sure.

Maybe in reading over them some day I'll find that out…Maybe I'll even figure out my purpose in life.

Until then….

2:15 a.m.

<Later> July 1, 2002

She asks me if I'm on heroine—If the marks on my arm are heroine tracks…of all that was serious about the night; about all of this…I can smile about that.

I guess it was only a matter of time before she would approach me—knowing something is wrong. She told me she was really worried about me and had been for a while. She said she could see a different look on my face. Which is interesting to me.

I asked her if she remembered the emails I sent her asking some crazy questions about suicide and stuff. This look came over her face then, and she said yes. It must have dawned on her then, I would guess. I said that I told her it was for the "book" I'm writing, and that was true, but I was also asking for myself.

She asked how long I've been in counseling and how it's going. I told her that I really like Mary (though I didn't use her name), but it's too early to know if any good is coming out of it....that it's been hard because I'm not used to talking in general.

So, I went home with her to help her paint her bathroom and...TALK. Scary for me.

She asked if I'd ever thought of taking it further. I said yes and told her she'd be surprised at how hard it really is to cut open a vein...It just kind of came out, and I think I scared her.

It's weird, but just thinking someone like Amy admires me is more than I can comprehend.

Speaking of Mary, she scared the shit out of me this past week. I don't know if I'm frustrating her or what, but she was talking about referring me elsewhere because she's not sure of her capabilities to treat my most severe traits...it's not that I can't understand that, but it scared me. I don't want to start over anywhere else or see anyone else. I don't want to be passed around. I just want her. I don't know why. I'm not sure why the thought of not seeing her anymore makes me so sad. I'll have to think about that. She stressed it wouldn't be "abandonment," that I could still go in and talk to her.

But I freaked anyway—in my quiet way. I just kind of sat there, looking down, breathing a little shallower, spacing in and out. I thought I might even tear up (!), but I didn't. I probably looked like an idiot.

What is wrong with me?

Well, that's going to have to wait for an answer...It's much too complicated for now. I must get to bed.

Besides, I don't know the answer.

July 2; an email from Amy.

First things first:

I hope you understand how much I care about you and worry about you. You are a dear friend. Friends...take care of friends....and I want you to know I am here no matter what you need.

I have been thinking more and more and I do have a few more things I want to say...or say again. So I will type them out here.

1) Please please please consider going to see Tonya. I think she can really really really give you some much-needed insight on this whole matter. I know you are concerned about money. But in the grand scheme of life...hitting a $250 dollar deductible for company-covered therapy is not really that much. That is less than 1.50 a day. That is less than a happy meal....YOU DESERVE TO BE HAPPY. You are not going to be TRULY HAPPY UNTIL you make yourself happy. YOU WILL NOT BE HAPPY UNTIL you find an inner peace. Spending $1.50 a day to find the help you need and deserve is WORTH you being able to move on in life with a fresh outlook. I know you feel like $10 a session is not bad. But remember you get what you pay for. Don't CHEAT yourself out of something you need and deserve. (did I say happy enough in this paragraph)

2) I honestly believe in my heart of hearts you need to take a few days off and spend some long time with your mom. If I were a mom and had a daughter in your situation...I would want to know. I know you don't want to put any more on your mom's shoulders...but she is your MOTHER. The woman who raised you. She has a right to know. You are closer to her than anyone else in your life...am I right???? If so....how can you go on hiding things from her??? If she knows you ...and is the closest person to you...hiding things from her will only make things worse. If you cannot have an open and honest relationship with your mom...who can you have an open honest relationship with???? A mother daughter relationship is the most basic of all....you need to nurture and develop it. If you keep hiding all these things from her...you are cheating her out of the

chance to be truly close to you...and you are cheating her out of the chance of trying to help you. Please please please consider this.

You may or may not end up confronting your father down the road...that is another bridge you will have to cross...but you owe it to your mother. You kept telling me "what difference does it make"...my question to you ...is how do you know what will happen until you try????

3) I believe in my friend....which has no true psychological training....that once you open up to your mom...and throw yourself more into counseling....your need to injure yourself with fade away. ONLY YOU CAN HELP YOU. You have a lot of people....(me and Trish for sure....) who will back you 100 % of the way. BUT YOU HAVE TO TAKE THE FIRST STEPS...and you have...and I am so thankful of that. Getting counseling was not easy...but you did it....it might not feel good now...but nothing good ever comes easy. You have to get past this so you can move on ...both personally....with relationships...and professionally.

4) Please know that you can talk whenever...about whatever...I can listen. But I am warning you...I am a tough friend. If you tell me you are going to do something....I expect it to happen. I care about you a lot....and want the best for you. I don't think any less of you...or think badly of you in any way. I admired you a great deal before ....for your tenacity—your determination...your spunk and your character. NOTHING HAS CHANGED. I have actually grown to respect you more for what you have gone through...and I look forward to really really admiring you even more...as I watch you go through this long healing process. I have always been honest with you...and I will always be. I only want what is best for you.

I feel like this is a really really deep email....please know I don't mean for it to upset or hurt you in anyway......I just want you to know I am here for you no matter what.

July 4

Mary gave me her home phone number and asked me to call her before I do anything to myself…a sweet gesture, but I can't imagine me calling her there. Just doesn't feel right. It's even hard to call at the office, which I did once and then felt really stupid about later.

The problem is—often it happens at night or really spontaneously or on the weekends. I would feel too bad to call on a weekend. I'm also not going to call at midnight or 1 a.m. either…but if I don't call, that might backfire on me eventually with this whole "referral" business…

July 7

I guess it all started after the fireworks on the 4th…

I got home late and though I was tired, I started working on [a dance routine]. It was so hot and I was tired and I couldn't get it right…it was really strange. I got so mad. In a way I hadn't been, or let myself, in years. I remember going for my razor, but not much else—Just that it hurt and that sort of brought me "back." Mary says I was dissociating. The cut was quite deep—deeper than any of my others ever before. I went on my wrist, right over the vein. None ever scared me before…but this one did. Weird.

spatter

one drop against
pristine white tile
spatters red my life

a little blood
seems a fair price to pay
for something that has
no value
a bit of blood
is a fair trade
for one full breath

a stream of red
hits porcelain white
spattering me into
a pattern of stained asylum

all of my blood
is an offering
lovingly spilled
if it means i'll drown
in the only beauty i know

5/04

July 14

So tomorrow I go to for an "assessment." Still scared as hell. Nobody better try to put me in any hospital…Mary seems to think whoever I talk to will decide what I need and give me options of people to go see.

I have to say I'm freakin' sick of making phone calls and going to see new people all the damn time.

I'm also a little nervous about the Wednesday meeting of the "Save Marissa Coalition." I actually started making a list of things I want to make sure I say. Make sure I get across to them…and I know this is one time I cannot mess around. They are taking time to sit down with me. I can't be shy, and I can't not talk. It's a real chance to talk. To people, women, who care.

I'm still pretty scared of that—to tell myself they care…because any one of them, or all of them, have the potential to pretty much break me by starting this out and not finishing…or sticking by me or making me feel they still care even months down the road. That will be hard to say to them, but I think it's an important thing for them to hear.

July 16

What a night. I could not have done that alone. I probably wouldn't have gone—and if I had, I would have taken one look at that place and promptly left. I felt numb walking in there. Wanted to cry while waiting…and several times during the "assessment."

The worst was when I looked over at Trisha, and she winked at me. For some reason, that just really got me and I wanted to just lose it….and again when I left the room so she could ask the lady something…I was terrified they'd come out of that room and she'd say she changed her mind, and I'd have to stay…that's a huge fear of mine. Being put in a hospital—I don't care how nice it is, and if I get to do crafts. I'm not going. I would go nuts in there…where cutting is not an option. And where I wouldn't have my house, my things, my sense of self.

What I went through last night…wow. When I think of how close

I came to having to stay…it blows my mind. That's very scary to me. So is the prospect of going to see an actual psychiatrist. I don't know why, but it seems so different to just go to a counselor than a psychiatrist.

***

I'd never been to any place like the clinic I went to that night. Just the word "clinic" was enough to freak me out. It was a really big place that seemed quiet and clean. I went there in the evening, so everything seemed really dark, too. I was taken into a small, but comfortable room, like a tiny living room. A woman came in a short time later and began asking me questions—a lot of questions. I don't remember what they all were. I remember feeling really small when I answered them, though. I remember feeling dirty and shameful, guilty and sad. But a certain sense of relief too, by talking about everything freely. I couldn't hold anything back. It just wasn't the time or place.

Eventually, the woman left to review my situation with her supervisor. I could only speculate on what they would do. I knew there was a chance I would have to be admitted. That scared me to death. I also knew there was a chance they could recommend some decent psychologists too. It was just a chance I had to take.

When the woman came back in, I held my breath. She was very kind and gentle, but she told me that both her and her supervisor thought I should stay where I could be monitored and have access to therapy at all hours. I know that Trisha thought I should stay too, but I just was not ready for that. I just could not bring myself to check myself in to a hospital.

I left the room after that so Trisha could speak with her alone. I waited, arms crossed around my middle, pressed against the wall, nervous. I watched people walk up and down the hall. I watched the secretary answer the phone and direct people to where they needed to be. I watched an older man come in the doors and stop at the front desk. He was balding and had a large middle. He had two suitcases that he sat down by his feet. I knew his was checking himself in, and the thought depressed me. I thought that could be me in a few minutes. I wondered how many people checked in and out per day at the clinic. I wondered what drove them to it, how long they stayed, did it help and how they did when they got out.

What would I be like after staying in this place for a few days and nights?

To this day, I'm still not sure what kept that woman from demanding I stay. She just took me at my word that I would be okay on the outside. Fool.

I guess other people thought so, too, because no one else tried to have me 302ed, including Tonya, who does that sort of thing all of the time. Her and I spoke many times about my cutting. She warned and she threatened, but she never acted. I'm not sure why. I don't know if she thought I was fine without intervention or if she thought I'd hate her guts if she turned me in. Maybe she forgot about it when I walked away. Of course I could never be sure I wouldn't open my door to find Tonya and her posse poised to take me in.

When I look back, I feel like I got away with something, like not getting committed was some sort of unpunished crime—a crime everybody knows about. I often wonder if anyone is sorry they never turned me in, but I try not to think how different things could have been if someone had. I'm not bragging that I got through things without that kind of help, because I almost didn't.

I'm just bragging that I got through it at all.

July 18
Wow. What a night. I have so many emotions, so many thoughts in my head...I have never been so touched...I'm sort of surprised I was so open and honest, can't believe that even though it was really hard to sometimes, I was still able to talk and say things.

July 18; an email from Amy after the "intervention night."
Hello there sweets!! You are very welcome. It was nice to talk and I just want you to realize how much we care about you. Tonya and I

spoke this morning. She said if you don't call her she will just wait for you on your porch step. She says she has a counselor who is excellent in these types of issues. (I don't trust work email that much) Anyway she said you can talk with her in conjunction with your other counselor. Please call her....she loves you.

Again how it all went down just so you know:

I called to get information. I kept everything anonymous. Then she said, "can I ask you—are we talking about Marissa." I gulped because I thought...okay, she called Tonya...so all is okay. Then she went on to say that [a friend] talked to her at Camp Cadet. And another too...but she did not tell me which one???? She wanted to call you the week after camp....but then didn't...because she was away....and then I called her that next Monday. Please don't be upset with me. I just knew she would have helpful resources. So please call.

You are so strong and so amazing. I can't wait for the day you look back on this....

I think it will be a life changing experience. Down the road I see you making a difference in other peoples lives....that is how strong and caring you are :) Just stare at your bracelet and remember we love you!!

July 21

I'm tired of making everyone cry. But I can't believe how much this is affecting them...when sometimes I don't feel it's affecting me enough.

July 22

People who know what's going on—Trisha, Amy, Jenn...I wonder if they think I hate life. I should have tried to let them know that's not true...I think I have a genuine love of life, as can be demonstrated by my desire to do as much as possible here, my feeling of wonder when I look at the ocean, my child-like playing in the water...it's all here...I wish they were here to see that.

July 27
The scars on my arm are beginning to heal. Not sure how I feel about that.

July 31
I had a Mary session last night. I don't do well with on-the-spot things. She asks for examples of things a lot. And I can either give them, but don't because they sound so stupid, or I can't think of any under pressure. So then it probably looks like I'm lying about whatever we're talking about. It's embarrassing.

And yet, I still go…I don't know what I expect to happen. It's hit or miss whether I feel better about anything…half the time I don't even know how I feel.

I haven't heard anything from [the clinic]. I can't decide how I feel about that. Relieved a little that I can stay with Mary. But unsure of what the problem is…I guess insurance issues.

I think Mary thinks they should have kept me. She says maybe they haven't sent her anything because they think they should have kept me too. I dunno.

August 2
She said I'm playing with fire cutting so much on my wrists. She said that's a free ride—a 5-day ride, to the hospital.

She says I deserve to be happy and have people care about me. I don't buy that yet. And she knows it.

She said something like "Happiness isn't an act, it's something you really feel."

I feel I should mention [the clinic] isn't as helpful as I thought it would be. I talked to a girl tonight who told me stuff I already knew about my insurance. I also thought they would give me some names and numbers to contact, but she didn't even do that…Dude, I'm so tired of getting the run-around. I don't think I can afford my insurance policy…and I don't know what to do about that.

Tonya says I'm going to find myself in over my head…actually, she says I already am. Is that true? I'm not sure.

I guess I am getting riskier with my wrists. And I wonder why…just to see how far I can go? I don't know if that's it….I have no idea why I'm there so often, not really caring…or thinking anything is going to happen.

August 3
I'm sick of [the clinic]. It's like…I'm okay with not having to go to anyone new just yet…It's so annoying to take time to call them…make an effort to do what I need to do…and get even more run-around. Every time I call, the person says she'll have to call back and she never does. And when I call again, that girl is never there, and I have to start all over again. Sigh. I'm waiting for a call now, when I could be doing stuff online. What I really want is someone to just give me some names of qualified people near me who can give what I apparently need. I guess I can do the rest. Then again, why bother. I can't afford my own insurance for these "specialists." This is ridiculous. And I'm deeply annoyed by it.

Okay, so the lady called me back—same one this time. But she didn't tell me anything I didn't know. She said something about [a service] here, but that costs 3x more than Mary and they're no different there…just a master's. So screw that. Maybe I should just go to [the clinic]. Screw the drive and just go there once a week. Good Lord—for all the trouble this is causing me…I'm tired.

August 7
I had to call Mary tonight, and I felt stupid. Nothing seemed real—it was like the newsroom and world were all a dream going on around me…happened before. She thinks I need meds. I don't want them.

Friday, August 16, 2002;
12:54 AM (A letter to my "coalition.")
My girls,
I debated about writing this email for a lot of reasons….I suppose I would prefer to do this in person since it is so sensitive, but I didn't

know when that opportunity would arise. It's much easier to share the good than the bad, so it would have been simple to just ignore this altogether. However, after everything I've put you through so far and everything you've done, it would be insulting to you to "hide." I guess I'm trying to live up to my part of our deal, though it's slightly late now, but as I mentioned before, I could have let it go completely. I had a minor setback last night, which is entirely my own stupidity and fault. The opportunity for help was literally in my face, but in the hopes I could get through it myself, I didn't reach out, therefore, paid the price. Although I probably would not have thought much about it, our dear Trisha would disagree. I turned to her because she happened to be there at the time; she has my "permission" to talk about it with you, (if you indeed want to) because it's not fair to hide it, and I don't want you to think I'm shutting you out after letting you in...that I don't care enough about you and consider you good enough friends. I feel badly enough about it all; actually, I feel everything about it from ashamed to angry to disappointed and sad. I know that I let you down, and even myself. And though it's happened before, and will probably in the future, I'm still working damn hard against it. It may seem hard to believe, but I feel you inside me and I hear your words, and it's helped on more than one occasion.

My main point in writing this was just to let you know what's going on, because you deserve to know, to tell you I haven't given up, but I guess need to try a little harder. For you and for me. Oh, and to say, once again, thank you for everything.

My love and heart,
Marissa

(A response from Amy)
Please don't apologize. I understand that this is not an easy road you are on. There are going to be speed bumps...and wrong turns.

My hope and dream is that you never ever have any setbacks....but I understand...and appreciate you sharing it with us. We can only help when we understand what is happening.

The point is this....you had the set back, you have addressed it…now it is time to put it behind and move on. You have already come so far….and each step will get easier…it just takes continuous drive and determination to get better….and if anyone has that drive it is you!

Take care sweets…and remember you can call anytime.

Love ya,

Amy

(A response from Jenn)
Rissa Rea,

It's only 9:35 a.m.—so I haven't seen our friend Trisha yet today. However, not knowing exactly what happened I still wanted to get an email out to you to let you know that you never have to apologize to me, ever. All I hope for you is that you continue to try to help yourself. And I'm not here to be hard on you when you have a setback…I'm here to offer you support and love from a friend. (if you want it or not)

Please be okay today and know you are in our thoughts. You are a sweet person who we adore.

See you later today.

Jenn

August 19

I'm in such a struggle with how I want her and Jenny and Amy to see me. I know the real me is the smiling, laughing, dancing one, and that's who I want them to see too. Most of the time, of course.

I don't want to appear too young and too immature and too vulnerable to them all the time. I really worry about that. So why do I keep giving them glimpses of exactly how I don't want them to see me? I don't get it. I'm such a moron.

August 21

I'm still a little frightened by all Tonya said to me last night.

I haven't even begun the healing process yet…WHAT? I was astounded by that. Really. If I haven't even started and it hurts this much and I'm as sick of it as I am...I can't imagine what the rest of this trip is going to be like.

She said she doesn't think I want to heal. It's pretty amazing how dead on she can be. I have to say, though, I'm not sure she's 100 % right on that on. I personally think I'm half and half and that's better than nothing at all.

I'm freakin' tired—all this "healing" is killer.

August 22; part of an email to Amy.

I met up with Tonya tonight; I just love the woman, but she threw a lot of stuff at me to think about and consider. She said some scary things...one being that I haven't even started to heal yet. WHAT? And I thought I was doing pretty well! Sigh...I just have to lace my boots a little tighter for a longer walk, I guess. She also said she's not entirely convinced that I'm ready and willing to heal....That's not the judgment from her that I want....But I guess she would know....Perhaps I have to work a little harder at convincing myself and therefore others? Yeah, I have no idea...all I know is my neighbors are doing some strange things out in the middle of the street right now, and I should go lock down my windows and doors!

(Her response)

I am glad you had dinner with Tonya. I don't understand your case as much as I would like to....but I do understand or at least some of what she is saying makes sense to me. How is the new counseling sessions coming along?? I knew you were waiting to get started. Please don't wait any longer....it is important that you get them under way....even if you can only go like once every two weeks or whatever. You are on a strong path right now....and you need to continue to follow it. I too have been a little confused as to why you haven't gotten it underway. I don't want to push too much....but at the same time I want to see you follow this through.

I don't want you to work harder at convincing anyone....I want you to work harder at actually doing it....when you are doing it and it is for "real" you won't feel the need to "convince" people......if you know what I mean…that sounds a little confusing doesn't it??? But I think you understand my drift?? We are all here to support you…. I am here anytime you need me. You know that….but I like to remind you every once in a while.

August 26
Mom and I had some good quality time together this weekend. It was fun. We talked a lot and did some shopping—of course!

I told her about my counseling. I was really nervous to do so. But I knew that I should. She said she wasn't hurt or upset that I talk to someone else. I don't know if she would tell me, though. We didn't talk too much about it. I was really tired, and didn't have much to say, really. And that's fine. I don't want to make it a big thing.

I didn't tell her why I go other than for work stuff and dad/baby stuff.

August 29
Last night I took a big step. I called Trisha late at night and asked for help.

It started in the shower…I cut once hoping that would be enough to get me through. But I just kept going. It was actually kind of weird. I've always been able to stop before. I wanted to keep going—more and deeper. It was really hard to put the razor down. But I did, I think because I was running out of room…

I was okay for a while after that, but then when I was sitting here on my bed later, I started again and couldn't stop. Even when I had a few deep ones, and they were still bleeding, I went right back at it. It was weird. I knew what I was doing, though. I just couldn't stop. Now I know how gamblers feel…It was scary.

I debated for about a half an hour to call Trisha. I thought about calling Jenny to give Trisha a break, but I worried about waking her. I was worried about calling Trisha, but I figured she would be more awake…besides, I was really thinking I'd get into some serious trouble if I didn't call someone.

I cut while I was on the phone with her, but after just a little, I threw the razor into the hall and stayed on my bed for a while.

It's not that she said anything, really. Just the distraction, I guess and from someone I love.

She didn't want to hang up the phone, so I did. I didn't want to go to sleep right away, and I was up every hour.

She kept saying at work how happy she was I called her. But that now we need to work on calling beforehand...The first call was just an icebreaker. And I guess so because it was pretty hard to do.

Her loyalty and patience is pretty amazing.

She must be getting pretty tired of me, though. Or at least that aspect.

I'm home from my Mary session. It was a strangely pretty good session...it felt like such a long time since I'd seen her. We talked about sexuality, then about my week.

While talking about it, I got a little nervous and sick, I guess. Lightheaded, like I could pass out...Mary noticed...she said I usually am radiant, but tonight I looked sallow. Sick. Like I needed to go to the hospital. Which launched a big discussion about what I ate today and anorexia. She said she's really concerned about it...

She said she felt like she needed to 302 me! She started ticking off the list of what's wrong; skin color, periods gone askew, denying treatment...

I think she's crazy—I'm nowhere near anorexia. She says she eats circles around me.

If I were anorexic, I certainly wouldn't weigh this much. I eat...admittedly, not a lot if I can help it. But that doesn't make me anorexic. She says she doesn't think I understand the dangers I'm putting myself in. She's right...because there is no danger. She says she thinks I'm starving.

She started talking again about going to someone else....no way. She said I should go to my doctor for a second opinion on it...I asked if that would make her happy, she said yes, so I said I'd go. And I told her I can't wait to tell her Dr. D. tells me Mary is crazy.

She told me twice that she really likes me and really cares about me...I was so touched by that, I can't explain why. It just meant a lot.

When I left and hugged her, I thanked her and she said, "my pleasure." She's so sweet.

But I still think she's crazy.

***

I was never anorexic. I would not even say I had a full-blown eating disorder. I just tried some different things to control my weight. Unsuccessfully, of course. We all know the correct and healthy ways to do that, which I try to do now. Thanks in part to my medication, I got my weight under control, and I'm happy to say, in answer to a previous question I asked myself in my journal once, I do weigh less than that 120 pounds I wondered if I'd ever weigh again. Go me.

But in all seriousness, I did struggle with my weight, even though I was by no means fat. I think for me, it was another way to punish myself, another way of abusing the body I hated.

Since I've been on my own, eating is not what I do best. I don't deny that I don't eat right. Sometimes I don't eat at all, sometimes I eat too much, but most of the time my food intake is probably just under the norm. When I first started trying to lose weight, I starved myself. That didn't last very long. I guess because to do the job I do, I needed some sort of food to give my body energy. So, I ate, just not a lot. After that, I started making myself throw up after I ate. But it wasn't like I ate a whole container of ice cream or a whole box of cookies, like most bulimics. Even if I just ate a few spoonfuls of ice cream, or a hot dog, it was into the bathroom, jamming my finger down my throat. I'm not a very good vomiter either. Not that anyone is, I guess it just comes out easier for some people. But not me. Half the time I'd start choking on my own puke. It would make my eyes swell shut and my throat hurt. It would come out my nose and make me sick enough to throw up again. Then, some time after it was all over, I'd be in the shower and more stuff would catch in my nose. Mary used to ask me at the beginning of every session; One, did I cut myself? Two, did I do any "purging?" She could usually count on a yes to each.

My family doctor, Dr. D., still asks me at my appointments, as well. Now I can answer no, but I'm not sure she completely believes me because I always start laughing when she asks.

But eventually, the whole purging thing was just too disgusting and draining for me. So, I wasn't a grade-A bulimic either. What to do?

I went to Dr. D. about the situation, after Mary asked me to. Dr. D. sent me to the hospital to go on this 1,200 calorie-a-day diet. Which wouldn't have bothered me, but it was just so hard to follow. No joke. There was all kinds of measuring and mathematical equating and planning. So, that didn't last long either. It wasn't that I was unhealthy. I ran (or jogged) just about every night, I was just unhappy with how I looked, along with everything else about myself. So, besides cutting, I found other ways to hurt myself, hoping they would make me feel better.

I know that I'm lucky I wasn't either anorexic or bulimic to the point where I seriously hurt my organs and health—like my cutting. I'm lucky I didn't end up severing tendons or amputating body parts. Or losing enough blood to accidentally kill myself.

People say eating disorders are a form of control for people, typically woman, who feel they don't have any. I think cutting or any self-mutilating is the same way. I used to argue with people that my body is my own, and I can do what I want to it. After all, people get tattoos, piercings, whatever. They sell it, inject drugs into it, dress it how they want....what's wrong with a few little cuts here and there? On my own property? I had control over my body, because it was mine. Nobody else could cut my arms or legs, just me. And nobody else could tell me that I couldn't cut. I had control over when I cut, where I cut, how deep I cut and how long I cut myself.

Just like the anorexic has control over how much she eats a day.

Both take incredible control. It was just too bad I didn't have that control to control myself against the cutting.

September 5

Okay—I'm sitting here at the gas station...just filled up. I've been filling up for years now...and I wonder what is our obsession with evenness? Why do so many of us top off to make it even? Instead of, like, $18.62...we go to $19, even if it means the gas overflows. But we're still satisfied because our credit card bill wish show an even 19 dollars, or we'll get exactly one dollar of change back from our even 20.

It's crazy.

But just try filling up and not topping off even—you can't do it because it drives you crazy.

September 6

What an exhausting session with Mary earlier...hard to explain. But telling her about some of the things I'm ashamed of...that was rough.

I only told her about the games I used to play with my neighbor, but I thought I would die doing so—and I couldn't even get it all out.

She asked me whose fault I thought it all was. I answered mine. And she said, no, it wasn't. She says I've got to forgive. Forgive myself...How exhausting and seemingly unreal to be able to do that—to comprehend doing that.

The guilt is too overwhelming right now. But I would love nothing more than to be free of it all.

September 7

This is a crazy book. It's way too much to read at one time...I never thought it would be when I started...and I never thought it would have the impact on me that is has been having. I don't know if that's good or bad?

September 11

She saw that I had been reading it and asked to look at it...I handed it over.

I watched her face as she read some of it—It probably looked a lot like mine when I read some of it. She asked things like whether a description of reactions or something was true. I think it was couple of reasons why we cut. I think she was sad when I concurred. She looked up the chapter on self-mutilation right away and read that.

September 13

I felt really stupid talking to Dr. D. about it. She's great, though. I liked how she didn't make a big deal out of looking at my arms...I wonder if she did glance when she was checking my breathing.

I wonder what went through her head when I told her.

I wish I could find a way to put into words how I feel when I leave Mary's. So tired. I'm already physically tired from the day. But then, all that talking, well, actually, a lot of listening. And I always feel so confused when I leave. About everything. But especially about trusting myself and my own intuitions. That always makes me feel bad too.

What would it be like to trust myself? I bet it's a nice feeling or at least a peaceful one.

Doing nothing with my life. This saddens me. What have I done? Okay, so I have a job. That makes me just like the 1073 kajillion people in the world who have jobs. Big deal. I need to volunteer somewhere or something. But I don't know if that's what I think I'm missing.

I know I want to make a difference—I just don't know with what. And that's just as sad.

I wonder who put that sermon in my mailbox. I'll have to ask Jenny tomorrow. But it was a good one. True too. But I wonder...whoever put it there...does she think I'm stuck in a cave? Or does she think I'm in the tunnel finding my way out? I sincerely hope it's the latter.

I wish I could be something/someone better.

September 16

I wonder if loving people as much as I do is an excuse not to love myself....as so many people say, you've got to love yourself too. Which I still find a ridiculous and unobtainable thing. But loving everyone else means I don't have to do it for myself. I'm not sure that makes any sense.

"The past really does shape us. But when we are ready, it is our own minds and our own will that help us re-shape until we are comfortable and pleased with our molding."
—an M.C. original!

I like to think I don't take any of my friends and the things they do for me for granted. Loving and embracing your friends is a big part of living and embracing life.

I only wish I could feel that way more often. I wish I could always feel how I do when I pause for a moment at night to make sure the stars are still there. Or when I look at the ocean or setting sun. How I feel when someone pulls me in for really tight, long hug. Or when I finish talking to God.

Contrary to perhaps popular belief, I love life…the little things of it, the quiet, sometimes hidden, things of it. And that's how I am…hidden until someone takes the time to look for me, into me…and while I think, or like to think, I give joy and make people happy, maybe it isn't until they really see me, all I have to give, that they feel how I feel about life.

I don't think that makes any sense either!

I wonder why it is so hard for us to always have such a happy, cleansed feeling inside.

Imagine if we did…how different our world would be. No hate. No fighting. God's love and miracles have the potential to create such peace…why can't we take advantage of that?

It's a September night—well after midnight. My CD player is going, playing music I've become a part of. Outside, the air is still, night creatures making their sounds…summer sounds we soon will forget as fall moves into place.

The streetlight casts its white essence onto the street.

I'm reminded of a scene in a long-ago short story—

The setting is much the same, but it's raining, the street flooded. The girl on the street is lost, tired, rain-beaten.

In slow motion, she turns in a circle, unsure which, if any, direction is safe. Lightening opens the sky up, but there are no answers there either. The streetlight illuminates her face, strands of hair sticking to her cheeks. Rain pounds the already flooded street.

The girl falls to her knees in the water, screams for someone to help her...but no sound comes out. She throws her head back, shouts at the darkened sky.

And now, in a flash of lightening, she sees...sees how that darkness wants to win. She's not sure she has the strength to beat it, but she'll die trying to.

The girl crawls, on hands and knees, cutting through the water...not knowing where she's going; only that moving what may be forward has to beat standing still.

From darkness to light, she moves.

(September 17, 2001 12:47 am)

September 19
In the world of flowers, I think a pansy most represents me.

It starts out dark in the middle, but its natural growth process unfolds its petals into bright, intricate, beautiful designs which hold the world's eye.

September 24
Where to begin? What a day. I really hate myself today. Some of it's left over from yesterday, but most of it is new—today stuff.

I really sucked ass at my two live shots...which never really sounds like much, but it's just such a big deal to me. I looked like hell, and my throat was acting up, so I sounded like hell too. I'm just really frustrated and disappointed in myself—I know I'm better than that. And to mess up with Amy on the anchor desk and Trisha behind the camera...and [a co-worker] sitting right there, no doubt laughing inside at me...It's not that I want to impress her. It's that I don't want to prove her theories that I suck...besides, I don't want to prove right my own theories of how I suck.

I know everyone has off days...but I always feel as though I should be excluded from the "everyone" category. Because I'm in my own. I just don't know where I could go from here even if I wanted to….No station is going to hire a sucky reporter.

It's a tough blow to me.

Anyway, I was so mad after my 5 that I actually stormed out of the newsroom and had to go do laps around the building. I haven't been that mad in….??? And I thought to myself, maybe I'm moving toward the anger stage.

Which apparently is supposed to be a good thing. But I'm not sure how because I freaked. I don't know what happened or why I got so crazy. I ended up in the bathroom…did just a few little cuts.

They decided I need to take kickboxing or something.

Might not be a bad idea. Especially if this is how it'll be if I don't find a way to handle these new feelings.

Anger. Never thought it was okay to feel it. Still don't. Don't even want to. Scares me.

All I know is I'm sick of messing up, and I'm sick of a lot of things.

I think I'm ready to start giving this up—I just don't know how to go about it for real.

September 25

But then she said she'd found a razor blade in her place one night…and I knew where it was going, but I made her say it anyway. Unbelievable that she would do that to herself—all in the name of understanding. She cut herself to understand. I'm not sure how I feel about that. At the time I think I was pretty surprised. I have a section like that I want to write in my novel; one of Madison's friends does it to see what it's like. I never thought one of my friends would try it. Like, how stupid! I looked at her arm—she did it on her forearm…not very deep, but I could still see the line. I didn't know what to say—what do you say to that? So, I asked if she got the understanding she was looking for. She said half and half…She could see how the pain could stop other things inside the head and heart. But she wasn't sure how anyone could do it all the time and deeper. She said it hurt "like a son of a bitch" and she realized I must be tough as nails. I don't know about that.

I'm not mad at her for doing it....I guess because I don't really have a right to be. I would be a hypocrite...because I say it's my body, I can do whatever I want to it. So, she can too. And I can't be mad that she cares that much and would go that far for my sake. That's quite amazing.

I'm quite certain I'd do the same for her or any other close friend...but to know someone did that just for me. It really sort of blows my mind.

Tuesday, September 24, 2002
9:55 PM (A letter to Amy)
[I] Also wanted to apologize for earlier today. Without getting into anything, really, I think I'm going into a different phase of things...and it's all new to me. Stuff I've never experienced or dealt with before, and I just don't know how to handle anything yet or where to put these crazy new feelings. Not that I knew before! But this is different. It kind of scares me...I've never been angry like this...or even had the slightest notion that it was okay to be that way. I'm struggling with it, especially if that is how it will be over the littlest things. It was a lot easier before!!! But I guess the easy way out doesn't cut it anymore. (pardon the choice of words). A lot of things set me off today, ending with the horrid display of journalism I had in my 5 and 6 live shots. I can't explain what it does to me when I don't do something up to the standards I set for myself...after being told over and over I'm nothing, when I mess up things, I remember those words and know they're true...so...that's always a trigger. I have a lot more to say, but this isn't the place....maybe next week, if that's an option? Besides, I'm really very tired, so this probably isn't making sense anyway. Just know that I'm sorry and that I'm still trying very hard....and that I love you very much.

(Part of a response)
I am very worried about you. I know this is part of the healing process...but I want you to remember we are here for you. We cannot

do this for you....God, do I wish we could....but we are here for you. You have to focus...you have to want this...and then follow your heart. It is not easy...and it probably won't get any easier any time soon...but very few "good things" in life are easy...just keep that in mind. By the way, I liked the poem a lot. You are an amazing writer....you can channel your experiences in an incredible way. I know this is very hard for you...but you have come so far....and you are moving forward. The best part of your journey is yet to come...I am sure.

Love ya,
Amy

September 26
I feel so crazy...but I've felt this way before. Sort of. I was angry again today...like I wanted to hit something, or break something. Break myself.

Everyone is so worried—Amy wrote me an email telling me such. She says I have to focus, to want it and to follow my heart.

God, do I want to. It's weird, but I can feel my heart...stuttering in my chest, ready to fly.

I wish I could figure out what is keeping it chained down.

October 7
She gave me my "surprise." A pair of fun boxing gloves! She has a pair too...She bought them just for me...well, us. Now whenever we're angry or whatever, we're supposed to keep them in our cars so we can beat each other and feel better.

We sparred for a little while last night, of course. We had to test them out! They're cool and fun.

But it's more than just having fun. I think I'm pretty tentative just yet—still such a scary thing to let go of my anger at all or at something other than myself. Plus, it's still my girl Trisha...I kept apologizing for hitting her hard or the wrong way. I didn't really let go because I couldn't, but because I don't know if I'd be embarrassed by it or not.

I mean, I was swinging and whaling away...I wonder what she was thinking. She said she wanted to make me angry....which is a good idea, I guess. Save for it being her making me mad.

Funny, though. Something as simple as just saying, "Come on, Marissa, get mad" or repeatedly hitting me in the face...did get me kind of fired up.

You've got to have a certain special kind of relationship to beat the crap out of each other and then hug when you're done.

October 10
Tonight/this morning, I'm feeling really anxious, really frustrated, even angry. Everything is making me crazy.

I feel like my life is out of control. And that's not good.

So, I just tried to simplify...simplify life. I cleaned out my filing cabinet. But I still feel cluttered. I still feel overwhelmed.

I'm like a crazy person...but I'm starting to wind down a little. But not really.

I wonder if now would be a good time to try some soap carving...Tonya gets my first attempt. Then my girls and then Mary.

***

People love to give suggestions—it's human nature. Even I love giving suggestions. It adds to a conversation and somehow it makes us feel better about ourselves—to think we help someone else with big or small problems.

Believe me, I've gotten my share of suggestions throughout all of this.

Something you have to understand, it's very hard for a person like me to hear some kind of substitution for cutting and immediately run out and try it. It's hard to imagine anything can work as well as cutting or drinking or getting high or whatever. Something else you've got to realize, nothing ever will work as well as cutting, or rather, *seem* to work as well because there's just something about it.

I've been known to scoff at quite a few ideas in my time.

One of the first I was ever given was to carve soap instead of my skin; compliments of Tonya. She told me maybe it was just the action of cutting I needed. She told me all about how her sister made her a duck one time and it turned out really well. I must have looked at her like she was a total buffoon. First of all, to compare cutting myself with cutting up soap? How could I feel better about myself by doing something like that? Second of all, art is not my thing. I can't even draw a stick figure. To boot, I'm a perfectionist. Trying to carve out a beautiful soap animal would make me want to cut myself more when it turns out like a piece of shit!

I did try it, probably twice. I can still remember the smell of that Jergen's soap I used for my first attempt. I looked at my razor blade and I looked at that small white bar. I felt like an idiot, but I did it anyway. I tried to make a flower—a daisy, I think. It's hard to describe what came out of it. It looked a lot like a kindergartener's drawing—like pencil lines rubbed in hard onto a piece of paper. It was a sad display of creativity.

I promptly turned it over to Tonya the next day. I never tried another soap sculpture again. I'm willing to bet I ended up cutting myself that night anyway.

That's not to say it was because the idea didn't work or wouldn't work for anyone else. It's important to try, even if you are convinced it won't work.

I did use some soap another time. Actually, I went through two bars of blue and white-striped soap that night. I remember clearly that I was at Trisha's house, trying to make it through one night without cutting. We did quite a bit: colored pictures, watched TV, tried some origami (which lasted about 30 seconds), I put on some music and danced around her living room, and then we finally hauled out the soap.

This time, using a knife, I didn't even think about making any kind of shape. I just launched in and cut that soap to pieces. They weren't even pieces—particles. I remember the give and smoothness the soap had, different from my own skin. I liked that feeling, thinking maybe if I pressed harder with my razor I could replicate it...not exactly what I should have been thinking, but I was. I remember taking my time cutting through the soap, wishing my skin could be cut up like that, shaved off.

When I was done, I had a large pile of it on a plate.

That plate sat in Trisha's kitchen for I don't know how long. I asked her what she was going to do with it, she said she didn't know, and then one day it just disappeared.

I was kind of sad to see it go. It was like a part of me.

Looking back, it's not really such a crazy alternative. I would even suggest it to others. And perhaps use it again some day when things are really bad.

Of course, it doesn't have to just be soap. Anything will do; wood, stone or rubber could probably do the trick.

The funny thing is, I later found that plate, with all of the soap pieces still on it. I dragged a chair over to her kitchen cupboard and stood on it looking for something. And there the plate was. It was weird seeing it. I pulled it out from the shelf, sniffed it, ran the pieces through my fingers. I put it back and hopped off the chair—just like that.

I've been told that maybe I simply needed the action of cutting, the simulation of the color red on my skin. So it was suggested I get some kids watercolor paint and streak my arms red with it. This came later on in the process, after I'd gone several months without cutting, and I was starting to think I'd break down and give in to the temptation to do so. It was a hard time because all I could think about was that blade tearing through my skin and blood and the satisfaction of it all. I wondered how the hell something like a child's paint set could take the place of the real thing. It irked me that someone else would think it could, even if that someone else happened to be my psychologist. I wasn't a big fan of that idea regardless of whether it would work or not, for reasons unknown to me. I never did try it, but I should have taken some of my own advice and just given it a shot. It couldn't have been more of a problem or hassle than actually cutting. Maybe it really would have felt as satisfying.

Other things I was told to try over the years....mostly things I like to do that would get my mind off of things. Obviously, writing was at the top of the list. Case in point: my journals.

Other things I tried....running. I call myself a runner anyway, because I do lace up the New Balance's at least three times a week. I can't say I really "enjoy" running. Usually while I'm doing so, I wonder *why* I'm doing so. But I always feel better when I'm done (done collapsing and gasping for breath, that is) It's weird, but I often get the urge to go out running. However, it's not one of the things that usually comes to mind when I'm struggling with cutting. It's just not a natural substitute, but that doesn't mean it's not one of the most effective deterrents. Everything comes out through your feet as they pound the pavement. You concentrate on pacing yourself, getting that next breath, which route you're going to take, the music and occasionally, the pain your body is in. By the time you get home, if you're not already dead, you're too tired to think about killing yourself. Now, this is just me talking, (and my sense of humor.) Believe it or not, I do have one, but I have to believe it could work for someone else too. There's nothing like dragging your fat ass into your place, sprawling on the floor until your breath comes back, then dragging your fat ass to the shower to wash it all off and start fresh. Not that the shower isn't a dangerous place, but I still believe that running sort of makes you forget all of that, if only for a bit.

Dancing is another thing that I relied on a lot. I am a dancer...much more so than a runner, that's for sure. Like running, there is concentration involved, but it comes naturally to me. I like it more. It's like pure expression. Not with words written or spoken, but the very body all of that emotion comes from. When I dance, nothing else is around me. And whatever is inside me comes out; through my expressions, a pointed toe, the reach of my hand, the extension of my leg. It's probably when I'm the most vulnerable, but most happy and at-ease.

Dancing is flexible, literally. But also because there are so many different kinds of dancing and so many different kinds of music to use. You can dance to anything for any reason.

When I'm angry, I can tap dance or do jazz to angry music. When

I'm sad I've got slow, lyrical music to use. Theatrical dance, hip-hop, Broadway, ballet are all fillers for however else I feel. There are so many options and so many ways to use my body and let go of my emotions. It's almost like I can never get enough of it.

When I lived in Bedford, I had the keys to a local dance studio just down the road. I used to love going at night. I didn't use any light but what came through the windows of the pizza place across the alley. Those were some of the most beautiful times of my life. Just me, the music, that light and letting go.

I would highly recommend dancing, even if you can't. Just put the music on, put yourself inside it and forget it all. Any kind of music, any kind of movement will do.

Like the blood that runs from your skin, so can the emotions run right from your heart.

Marissa's List of Alternatives

1. Write
2. Run
3. Dance
4. Break dishes
5. Beat on a tree with a bat
6. Play racquetball
7. Scribble on paper with crayons
8. Paint yourself
9. Beat on a punching bag
10. Sign up for some kind of martial arts
11. Step-aerobics
12. Chainsaw art
13. Soap carving
14. Bang some pots and pans around
15. Go to the batting cage
16. Go to the driving range
17. Hammer nails into a board
18. Throw darts
19. Join a bowling league

20. Shred paper
21. Hold pieces of ice in your hand and let the water slide down your arms
22. Wear wrist bands; they feel like the gauze you get after you've been stitched up

1:59 a.m.
She says she's never known me to not do something I put my mind to. The pressure is on! Sort of. I don't want to let them down. Do I want to let myself down? That's a tough one…no. Of course not. I'm just frightened to move beyond it. I guess that's it.

For once in my life, I'm not sure I have the words to explain anything I'm feeling right now.

It's now 2:39 a.m. I feel a little calmer. But very restless. Still anxious.

So, I feel like nothing and like I'm dying. Not a good combination. The deepest parts of me feel empty tonight/this morning.

3:30 p.m.
I'm dying…I'm just dying. I'm losing it too. I'm losing my mind and my sanity…and all I can see is my blood all over the place. I can see me cutting my wrist so deep, so hard…I'm sort of shaking…and I feel like I'm completely crazy.

I wonder why in the hell people get started on drugs or anything addictive in the first place—or why they ever choose to quit.

This sucks. Am I ever going to feel normal again?

Or better yet…when will I want to feel what real normal is. Want to stop putting myself back in that place that drives to this point as it is?

That made no sense.

When will everything I felt/feel when I cut stop feeling normal. That may be a big help…

I wish I could just run…run forever, run until I can breath normally, run until everything strips away from my outside and the true, real, and improved Marissa takes flight.

Flight. Fly. On new wings. Whole wings.
I want that. I do.

October 13; an email from Jenn.
Rissa,
I want you to know that I am so proud of you. You're stronger
than you think. Look at what you've been challenging yourself to do
this week, and how fun and alive you were Saturday night, despite
your own personal struggles. Truth is, I admire your strength. When
life is good, it's easy to be happy and smile in a crowd, but when life
is tough, it's not easy, and you brighten up a room— despite your
inner struggles. Keep going…you're more than 1/2 way! Love ya.

October 14
This sucks. I never want to do this again…I'm not even doing it
for me anymore. I'm doing it for them. I doubt that's the way it should
be, right?
Later
I talked about this with Mary, who says it's normal—many
people "recover" not for themselves, but for others. When I think
about it, I guess it makes sense.
Some of us care more about others than ourselves…so we care
about letting them down, and their feelings.
Trisha has told me so many times how much it would devastate
her if I killed myself. The people-pleaser in me couldn't stand to hurt
her that much, especially after all we've been through.
I couldn't picture myself doing that to my mother. My God, I
can't even tell her about any of this for fear of crushing her. So
imagine…well, I can't even imagine.
Will I ever see this as a reward for myself? I don't think I should
be rewarded.
I have to admit, I cut today—in the shower. I guess I could have
held off…but I didn't…I cut once because I could. Then I felt bad
about it, so I cut again…and then again…and I had a hard time
stopping, and I wanted to go deeper and fill my bathtub up with

blood…and I was right back where I started….

I felt bad about cutting the first time because of everything I put my girls through. How disappointing to go 5 days and then be too weak to keep going with it.

Did I let them down? Probably—and they don't even know it yet. Did I let myself down? I guess so, but I don't know why yet. I guess when I figure that out, I might be more on the road to recovery…when I don't want to let myself down anymore.

October 16
If there's anything in this life I don't take for granted, it's the awesomeness of being on my own and living my own life. Just tonight, I was getting batteries out of the van—a perfect October night. Chilly and rainy. My neighbor was just getting home too, and we chatted through the stairs. Something as simple as that…

So live every day as though it's your last…you only pass this way once. Do it right.

By God, I'm trying.

Scars remind us the past is real.

That they do. But they also give us the choice; to live there in the past, held captive by that power….or to see them for what they are. A past that has shaped us, but a springboard to a future we shape ourselves.

October 17
I have this image in my head…of showering, and of blood.

I can't explain how cool it is to see the water turn red, to see the blood fill up my palm, cover my hand

October 17; an email from Jennifer.
Truth is, I think it's great that you are a writer. For one, it's fun (I like to do it) and it's a great way to vent your thoughts about things—and a bonus to get to read them later when you're in a new phase of life. We've talked about this before, so you know what I mean. But I also really think it's great because I can see you down the road

117

helping someone else by sharing your experience with your writing. You're a great writer, and as hard as it is—I'm glad your recording this challenging time in your life. Thank you for sharing your personal story with me.

October 19

Words could never do it justice, which is annoying because I want to explain what's in my head. And while it won't completely fade away, it will never be as clear as it was seeing it...

So many emotions, feelings. But not one of them bad. Except maybe sadness that it will come to an end.

But...wow. It's complete peace. Total calm. Happiness, joy, blessed. Relaxed.

It's amazing. I saw so much today—and not just saw it...but saw. I saw a chance, really an option, to start over in a way. Begin again the way I want to.

Waterfalls...gotta write about those—the way they look, the way I looked at them and wanted to be them in ways.

All I can really say (write) right now is how happy I am...how free I feel.

October 20

So, now it's time to head back to reality. Although I sort of have to argue that point...that what we saw yesterday and did yesterday was the actual reality of this world.

That's what it's all about, really.

The most basic form of everything—most basic form of nature, of where we all come from.

That's reality. Not deadlines and pressures, cell phones, pagers, leads and breaking news. Not violence and drugs and murder and abuse. That's the surreal of people, too busy, too sheltered and too crazy to take it all in, to see and really understand.

We saw so much beauty....natural beauty yesterday. None of it looked the same...it was simply amazing. And I had to thank God for it...and thank God I've never really taken any of it for granted ever.

That's no way to live.

It's so hard to explain how I felt being so far into nature, looking at those incredible gems God created in the middle of it all. Nothing slipped by me, went unnoticed, went without thanks. I looked at it all, saw it, breathed it all in to make it a part of me.

We talked about it on the way to [our destination]…I felt so free, so uplifted, so new and complete there. I thought to myself—this is the perfect time for a new start, a fresh beginning. That's how it made me feel—like I'm ready for a new start, that I'm worth one, that what it all comes down to is the gem God put inside me. My own waterfall in my heart and soul. It's an amazing feeling.

We talked about the path water takes to get from mountain to river…Choose your path.

We talked about how people just don't take the time to enjoy the "simple pleasures," the "simple happiness" of life. We feel sorry for them.

All that matters is how much fun I had and what I brought home with me from the trip.

I hope to hold on to all of it with everything I have, and turn to it at my low points.

After all…"Just when you hit rock bottom and come to terms with how beautiful it is, it's the journey back up that really counts."

November 14

At any rate, I'm going out of my mind today…I'm not sure how much longer I can hold on.

I had a "night" last night in the shower…I hadn't cut like that in a long time, and it felt so good. I wanted to do more and more…deeper, of course. My shower looked cool, and I have a cool thing on my wrist….

It's so easy to slip back.

It's my own emotional stupidity and insecurity that led to the cutting.

I may do some more today, I may not. I just don't understand myself. I need to toughen up…but I know that I can't.

It's way past time to let last night go…breathe in a new day, put myself in a happy place.

November 30
Interesting to note:
I started counseling May 16, 2002. Just a year after I started at [the TV station]. It'll be a year of counseling in May. Two years here at [the TV station].
How far have I come?

November 31
I just saw a commercial for the Ronald McDonald house—all those sick kids. It makes me sick that I sit here in my place of inconsequential things, material things, and look around, smiling at it all because it's mine and because I love it all.
When people are dying and crying all over the place…why am I so lucky and blessed with health and everything I have? Why am I so lazy that I don't find any way to help or make a difference? I really am a bitch.

December 3
On my way home, I had a very profound experience.
I was getting off the exit when I saw a very bright shooting star streak green through the starry night sky.
It was really beautiful…I got all emotional…thinking it was a sign from God—that He is watching and caring and will take care of things.
It was a really great feeling.

December 15
I've been thinking a lot lately about dance. It's certainly no secret I come alive when I dance. It's my "passion" for sure. And teaching too. I really miss that…I often wonder if that's really what I'm supposed to be doing…my own studio. I remember before I started college, that's what I wanted to do…study dance and business.

That's all I know how to do...dance and write for fun. I remember Mom talking me out of it. She said what would I do with a studio...working nights, no health insurance, etc., etc. I think I still harbor some resentment toward her for talking me out of it...not supporting that dream of mine.

Life takes one to crazy places...for reasons, I like to think...I look at all the people I've met because of my career path, all the things I've learned and seek...but especially the people. And I wouldn't change any of it...no way.

Then I wonder if my life went that way to meet who I met, and now it's time to take a new turn down that passed-over dirt road? But then again, how do I just career off the road I'm already on and the trail I've already blazed. Everything I worked so hard for and learned and do now...how do I give that up?

They say the greatest risk is not taking one, nobody ever said you have to stay on the path and all of that...

What if I already did take my risk? What if I changed everything and realize I made a huge mistake by doing so? Oh, the uncertainty!

I guess when, or rather if, I'm ever ready, I'll know. By then, it could be too late! Dancers don't last forever...I'm so confused.

I feel very confused right now about something else...

I knew all along how easy it would be to slip back...I went one month and three days...but I lost it all tonight.

Four little ones...I was shaking—literally shaking. I was crazy—going through drawers looking for something, anything to use. I ended up using a steak knife...and I'm so unsettled right now because I want to keep going...I want more, I want them deeper...I want blood all over the place. So, what is holding me back? I don't know, other than I'm here at Trisha's and she'll be home soon, and I guess I don't want to deal with that...which is a sorry excuse. More like I'm just a baby...but truly, I don't want to make a big scene. I should have stayed home...I had done so well. I don't know if I feel bad about this—I think I'm too crazy right now to worry about it.

I really feel like I'm on drugs...I'm still shaky because I want more...I should have started it earlier.

Okay. I feel little better. I can breath a little now. I created enough pain to bring me down some…Still a little shaky. I wish Mary were here…

I wish I weren't here.

I don't understand…I change so quickly. So quickly. It's really weird. I had so much to write about…I don't want to write anymore.

Yet I have nothing else to do…but write. I would go for a run, but I don't have my shoes.

I would go for a dance, but I'm not home and I don't have my shoes—those damn shoes. Trying to find humor. I can't.

I'm going crazy. Really really crazy. I…want my shower…my razor…a red bath tub.

I'm sitting right next to her and I can't even say anything. I can't even ask for help. I'm frozen. Locked inside myself…trapped. Going insane…and going there all alone. I can't speak, can't move, I'm shaking, just my hand is working…Oh, God. The tears are coming. Welling up in my eyes…make them stop. Make all of this stop.

Just go away…If I don't keep writing, who knows what I'll do…but I want to do it so badly.

Wish I were alone, then I would.

I can't take this much longer, mental hospital? Okay. Just kidding about that. I don't even think this is really me writing any of this. I don't know where I am…still locked up. Trapped. I can't get out…Please help me find my way out. I'm scared. So scared….and alone.

And so tired. God, I'm so tired.

December 16

I'm afraid to read what I wrote yesterday….So I think I'll hold off.

I always mess things up.

It's hard to explain the night….I cried, actually cried. Hard. Like I haven't in…I don't even know. It was scary for a while. But then…it felt good. Even though I couldn't stop for some time. I felt out of control crying like that…but I guess it's better to be OOC [out of control] that way than doing anything else….Even though I may want to. And I know I won't always be able to cry. I may never again. I don't know.

But it was a scary night.

I'm getting there….this was bound to happen. It could have been worse…and while I still struggle mostly with wanting to and knowing I shouldn't, I know I have to be getting better. A few months ago—I wouldn't have thought it was wrong at all.

This is hard enough—but everyone wants me to tell my mom. I'm so not ready right now. The thing is…will I ever be?

Kinda like asking if I'll ever weigh 120 pounds again?

Unanswerable.

December 31, 10:19 p.m.

The last few hours of 2002. Geez. I don't think this year went by too fast. But it didn't really go slow either….It's weird.

I try not to get into the whole "I'm glad this year is over" or whatever mood.

A new year, a fresh start….but every day is a fresh start, really. No year should be looked upon as worth leaving behind or a waste. Now, I admit…2002 was not my best year personally.

In fact, it had the lowest points of my life in it…which I need to let go of—not the year. A lot of really great things happened in this year…

It was a year, you know? That's all. A new one is about to begin— and I hope it's filled with love, joy and peace for me, family and friends.

New Year's is dumb.

But I can definitely understand why so many people kill themselves during this time of year.

I think my cutting tonight had to do with a lot of different things— just depression over the holiday season which comes regardless.

General depression.

A general hopelessness about life…my depression, the things that are going on in my life right now…

I gave in, but I guess it's better to do so now, in the hopes that I can leave that behind with 2002 and start the new year clean and fresh.

I know it won't be easy—it hasn't been so far. I can hope, though, that the good and pure in my heart can win this year...my strength wins out.

January 10, 2003

I'm horrible...way too long since I've written. It's so hard to admit, but I don't feel like anything has changed. I miss the person I used to be...the happy girl who never let anything get her down...

I'm really tired—so tired of this unhappiness and mixed-up feelings and confused heart. I just want it to end. I have this vision—of everything coming out of me—like the rainbow I described in my novel.

Or me, walking out of the black that has swallowed me...the sun shining brightly, a sort of halo all around my body...eyes bright, skin glowing, feeling so free and light. No memories, no heartbreak. Nothing but a love for life and what the future has and nothing particular about the past. Just that. The past—a past I can let go of and release.

February 8; an email from Jennifer

As always...thanks for sharing your most inner thoughts. This part of your entry made me want to reach out and hug you and hold onto you for a long, long time. While there may not be any going back—you are not alone on your travels. Please remember that always. And make sure that we (your friends) are doing all that we can to get the lonely and scary feelings to go away. You're not alone, Marissa. Friends are a wonderful gift. They make sure that you never feel alone, that you always have someone to talk to and they make sure you have someone to laugh with. You do all that for your friends...make sure we're doing that for you.

When I think about the 1st night we 3 girls got together and talked at Amy's house I realize that there is already a big difference in you. I'm so proud of you and the progress you have made. Don't let yourself feel lonely, Rissa, and don't be afraid. You do have the strength to be okay.

Love, Jenn

February 25

It's terrible that I never write anymore—now that I'm "stable," I don't write.

If you want to call it stable. I'm just doing better, I guess. If you catch me on a good day!

I'm finally breaking down and asking Dr. D. about anti-depressants. I had a very profound moment one day where I realized....I can't do it on my own anymore. I have no control over my emotions and it's ridiculous when I can do something about it.

I don't want to feel how I do anymore, so I'll try to fix it....

Sad for no reason...incredibly sad, despondent and depressed. Crying, teary-eyed. It's awful.

And it kind of gets in the way of work and life...

It's weird how fast opinions and decisions can change...a few months ago, I was adamantly against meds. Now I can't wait to get them and try them out...hope to God they work.

Charlotte described it pretty good—"with meds you can at least have ground under you." With ground, you can start to put your emotions in order, at least. That thought is very appealing right now....

I'm anxious to see how it works. Maybe I'll loosen up a little too. Because isn't that what everyone wants?

I Am a Man

I am a man, he says, and I have needs.
    But your wants are no different
    From your needs, and you want something I need.
I am your friend, she says, and I have needs.
    But your needs are the same as his wants
    And I don't want what you need.
I am a man, he claims, and I want you with me.
    But you don't need what you want
    Like you want what I need.
I am your friend, she claims, and I want you with me.
    But you want what he needs
    And I don't need what you want.
I am a man, and I need you.
    But you only need what you want
    And I can't want what you need.
I am your friend, and I need you.
    But you only want what you need
    And not what I want.
I am a man, and I want you.
    But you want me to need guilt,
    And I will not want what you need.
I am your friend, and I want you.
    But you need me to want hurt,
    And I will not need what you want.
I am your lover, they say, and I need you to want me.
    But your wants have nothing to do with my needs,
    And I don't care what you need me to want.
    Because nothing is what I need,
        And nothing is what I want.

April 14
I've quite literally turned a new page.
A new page in my journals of life….a new page in life.
It's almost too much to go into now, since I've spent more than 5 weeks trying, not to forget, but to learn and move on.
To turn my back on the darkness, and instead, follow the light I've chosen to reignite in my heart.
It's amazing, really…the transformation, the metamorphosis that has begun. I'm not even sure those words are strong enough—truly describe what I feel inside these days.
The issues are still there, I still have things to process, still have healing to do. But now, when everything is out, I have so much total support from my mother, my love, my friends…when everything seems so new and fresh, when I have some crazy new outlook on it all….
It's just neat.
I haven't cut in 5 weeks and 2 days…I haven't even wanted to…save for yesterday—my sister's first birthday.
That's a really nice feeling too. Not cutting. Toward the end—I really didn't even want to. It just happened by compulsion. Now that I am realizing I don't need that, it's not really who I am or what I deserve, that I don't need blood to feel better…I realize…hey—I don't need it. It doesn't make me feel better anymore. It actually made me feel worse, and it hurt so many people. Even me—which I now know.
I'm just sorry it…no. I'm not sorry, I guess. Because it happened for a reason; It was bound to happen.
I'm just sad it took 25 stitches to put life back into my soul.
After all….life is our greatest gift—and I hate to look back and think I wasted even one second dying before my time.

April 15
The more I think about it….the more I fear looking back and regretting anything.
Everybody has regrets in life, I know that. Sometimes there

doesn't have to be regrets…Some things don't deserve regrets.

So that's why I'm trying to really get past all of this.

Know and realize what happened…process it, learn from it…and move on being a better person for it.

I look at my arm now and I don't see the "proper" markings anymore. I don't see cool lines of damage, what shows the world I'm damaged. I don't remember fondly the blood that dripped from them—sacrificing myself for something so totally stupid, something I could have just as easily dealt with by taking up whittling or something.

But then again, it was never really that easy. Much as I'd like to convince myself of that.

I just skimmed back through some of my old entries, and I feel like such a hypocrite with some of the things I wrote—about life being new, blah blah.

So as I write all these words, it just seems like a big lie.

Another spin on the merry-go-round—and today, I just happen to be back at the beginning.

I can honestly say, though, that each time I wrote all that stuff, I truly meant it…It felt real….

Like now. But now is different somehow. If that makes any sense. It's weird.

Sometimes I think I'm so in control of everything, so leveled out…and then sometimes I feel like I'm spinning out of control on that merry-go-round. For no reason. I'm afraid I'll never stop.

I used to be dead-set against medication. Why…I'm not sure. But I finally had to break down and get it…

April 17

And now that I have it, I'm really glad.

I do think it helps….I don't know how, but it does. As Charlotte described, it gives me a ground to stand on. I didn't have any ground before—an endless, bottomless fall when I started falling.

It's not a miracle drug—It doesn't keep you from never feeling sad or depressed…but it slows the descent down and lets you hit some kind of bottom along the way.

Which I think is just great. For a while…I forgot what it was like to be happy….To be myself—how I used to be.

And I missed that a great deal. I missed myself.

The weird thing was, after I started the meds, and things were getting back on track, I forgot what it was like to be sad.

The first day I was—just because that's human nature—it hit me hard. I didn't like it and couldn't believe I'd spent so many days feeling that low.

People say you can't love others if you don't love yourself…Hmmm. I forgot where I was going with that one.

Oh well. Medication rocks.

April 18

I finally got to start *Prozac Nation*. It's really good so far. Weird how I can relate to parts of it. It's like, I read something, and I'm like, "Yes—that's me!"

Interesting how that seems to help more than a professional book.

April 19

I have to admit the process of finding a new counselor is killing me.

Nobody calls back, or if they do, they are booked until June or not in until May or it's not their specialty. How annoying. I mean, really.

When you actually try to get on the road of recovery, it's like trying to part the Red Sea.

I'm so tired. I just put my head down and fell asleep. Holy cow. See what work does to me?

April 24

And now I am 25.

A quarter of a century.

But it's a good feeling.

I find it odd, yet inspiring that it is the first year I'm not looking back.

Birthdays are kind of like New Year's—I've always held on to the last seconds of one year instead of looking brightly ahead to the next one.

It's not that I didn't look forward to my birthday—but I guess there's a fear of aging, a fear of the future. I wish that weren't so—especially since there's so much of the past I want to let go of.

This year, it's all ahead. I'm looking at it optimistically. Ready (sort of) for the challenges and ready for all the fun things that make up life.

It's interesting. I wonder why this year I'm so positive? Is it because I feel so free these days? Medication? Or is it really becoming an age thing?

I don't know, and I guess it doesn't really matter.

All that matters is how I feel—and that's good. Excited.

Twenty-five seems like a good number. I will say that I'm really enjoying my 20s. They are pretty good ages.

I still fear the future a bit—because that's just who I am, I guess.

I fear more simply because of the situation I find myself in.

At the same time, I'm so ready to move on, move forward….Other people still manage to hold me back.

With gossip, rumors, back-biting…human nature.

I'm just so tired of it all. I will never understand why people care so much about everyone else's lives and personal business. Then to talk about it all like they know everything about it, like it's their business….it blows my mind, and I wonder why more people can't see it my way?

It takes so much energy to spend that much time speculating about everyone else.

It's energy I don't have. Nor care to expend on stupid stuff. Like other people who aren't important to me.

Still trying to crawl ahead and find the joy, humor and beauty in life.

And maybe pass it on to everyone else somehow.

April 25
In reading *Prozac Nation*, I've come to realize….how horrible a thing depression is. Not just the regular blues or depression after breaking up with someone.

But the real thing. The endless, desperate, painful kind. Clinical depression. I realize I have that to be thankful for—I don't have that, I haven't gotten that far. I've been seriously depressed, so I can relate to some of what the author writes. But what I can't relate to seems like pure hell.

For the afflicted and everyone around her.

It's a really good book, and I think I want to get my own copy. Like a reference guide, sort of.

I think I'm depressed. Isn't it funny? Even with pills, I can still get depressed.

I think that's the hardest thing to get used to—they aren't a cure-all. They don't make you happy and relaxed and full of life all the time.

They don't fix everything. Even though I've written about it before—I forgot, so I'm writing about it again.

Because it is true. And it is a big deal and adjustment when you start them.

And when I'm miserable, I still feel pretty miserable. But I know I'm not as miserable as I would be without the meds.

Today, I'm not completely miserable. I just feel sort of lost. A little empty inside and a little desperate.

For what, I'm not sure.

I'm really tired today. I really just want to go back to sleep—under my covers, close my eyes, travel away from here.

One of these days, I guess.

I wonder how much of my medicine makes me tired…the extra pill. Maybe I'll get used to it.

April 29
Oh, how I'd love to be "cured" of everything. Everything.

Cutting, depression, crying, sadness…I know life is never easy. But how much easier life would be if all were cured.

I think of that all the time. If I accepted drinking, thought it was cool and funny like Trisha, how much easier it would be. How smoothly things would go, and how much less irritation I would feel.

How much I would feel as though I fit in.

While it seems so easy, and I feel like it would be better, whenever I think about it....I get sick in my stomach. Because it's not me. I don't agree with any of it. I don't want to be one of those people who do.

I don't want to find humor in drinking until you're acting like an idiot. I don't want to think it's cool to waste hours in a bar. Waste good money on drinks.

That's fine, but I can't understand why I can't stand it. I don't understand why I have no patience, no understanding, no tolerance.

And I guess that's why I'm really wishing I had.

I don't have to agree or even understand...but at least tolerate it all.

I wish I could figure out why I'm so hung up on it. It takes so much energy to be this way. I hate it all. I hate that part of myself.

March 26; part of an email to Tonya:

Things here are going well. I debated whether to tell you this, but figured I probably should since you've been helpful during the whole ordeal....It is hard for me, though, because the whole thing upsets and embarrasses me. About three weeks ago, I wound up in the emergency room and needed a fair amount of stitches in my arm. It was a terrible night, but one that scared the shit out of me, which may be a good thing. Since then, I haven't cut, nor have I even wanted to do so. I am switching counselors; I will be starting with a psychologist in the near future...once I get things straightened out with insurance and my family doctor. I've been on anti-depressants since that night. I surmise they are working. The change, I must admit, is amazing. You may be happy to know that my mom came up after that for a few days and we had a few long talks. We are now on the same page with everything, so that has helped tremendously, as well.

I think it's sad and strange how things work....It took something so horrible and so hurtful to so many people to completely change me around. Thank God that I have such wonderful, loving family and friends. I haven't lost them with my actions, and they've been nothing but supportive. It's hard to explain the change I feel inside me...but I know that it's there. And I'm so damn glad. I've wasted enough time, eh? Only one way to go....and that's forward. It probably all sounds like crap to you...and that's fine! I just wanted to let you know what's been going on. Like I said, I wasn't sure I would/could....but you deserve to know. And besides....you are cool.

March 31; part of Tonya's reply
You know darn well it doesn't sound like "crap" to me—I care very much about you. I'm sorry that it took something so drastic to bring about the change, but I'm grateful for it. The thing that you felt helped you cope turned into something very dangerous for you. I knew that it would take something to make you give up your attachment/dependence on it, but I could not have predicted what or when. I'm just grateful that you're still around to talk about it. I'm also very glad that you and your mom had a few long talks—I assume that she turned out to much more supportive than you ever imagined. Lifting the shroud of secrecy is a good thing. Remember—you're not the bad or guilty person here. Switching counselors is a good thing too, as is the medication. Sounds like you're starting to move forward instead of treading water.

***

For a long time, I knew there would come a time I'd have to write about "that night." The night in March when I ended up in the emergency room. At first, it was simply too painful to even think about, let alone write about. Then, it was embarrassing. There are some things I'm sure I don't remember. I don't know what I looked like to my friends, standing there, watching this whole thing unfold.

A big part of it all is that I just didn't know how people would react to what happened. Would they at least see a small part my way? Could they even begin to understand why it had to happen? Even writing this now, I have fears and worries. But I can't write my story without including the worst and most painful event.

Trisha and I took a small vacation to Virginia Beach to visit friends who had moved away in March. I was nervous about going anyway because, quite frankly, I am not that great with big groups, social settings, partying and drinking. It's just not my scene and I feel very uncomfortable in such situations. I knew that my "vacation" was going to be mostly those things. It's a lot like those cute little Zoloft blob commercials; I'm the blob, blushing and sweating and wishing I were anywhere but where I am at the moment.

I thought I had prepared myself for it, and for the first 24 hours, I think I did pretty good at containing myself. I tried to forget all I was dealing with personally; tried to forget about my woes at work, my family life and the torment inside of me. Saturday night, it all came out—more like exploded.

After a long dinner, a group of us headed to a bar for dancing and more drinking. By that time, I know that Trisha had had enough of me. I was not having fun, and I was not the best of company. I knew it then, and I know it now.

Also by that time, another friend Sam, was sick of me too, telling me I wasn't the same girl he knew when we lived in the same town, which is true. I wasn't the same because I was going through so many changes and so many different moods.

He and I had a small exchange of words, then I told Trisha that I wanted to leave, at which point, she got upset with me, which escalated into a full-scaled fight by the time she, Jesse and I packed in the car. Sam refused to ride with us and instead walked home with a friend.

Trisha was screaming at me to "never point your fucking finger in my face again," and suddenly, the overwhelming feeling of guilt hit me, full on.

I felt selfish for demanding to leave and horrible for behaving like a slug while I was there on vacation. I felt scared because Trisha had never yelled at me like that before. I was also scared because I could feel something welling up inside of me that I'd never felt before. I didn't know what it was, but I knew it was serious. I felt like I was losing control. Everything I'd held inside of me for long, everything

I was dealing with and everything that was happening that night was overflowing. Boiling. All of my emotions were starting to mix together and they were so intense I couldn't keep a cap on them.

Trisha and I fought the whole way back to Jesse's apartment and when we got there, I was ripped open. That's the only way I can describe it. I don't remember what I was thinking, but I know that I pulled the razor out of my jeans pocket, looked at Trisha and sliced through the skin on my wrist. Once, twice, three, four, six times, I'm not sure. I didn't feel anything. I really didn't even see anything; a veil was over my eyes and my mind. I don't know what made me stop, but when I did, things came back into focus.

I saw Trisha in front of me, her face dark red, her eyes bright green with tears running down her cheeks. It was horrible to see her like that—so mad, so hurt, so confused. To this day, it's one of the most painful things of the whole incident.

She screamed to Jesse something like, "Do you see what she's doing? Do you see?!" Jesse peered at me and asked, "Why do you have a razor? Why would you do something like that to yourself?"

Trisha said something like, "She's doing it to prove a point to me." I do understand why she would see it that way and why she would say it, but she was far from the truth. At that point, it wasn't anybody, I wasn't proving any point, I was just coping with stress and hurt the way I always did— by cutting. I was so far gone that I couldn't have even come up with a good reason for doing it, or anybody to blame it on. I didn't even really know what I was doing.

The next thing I remember is Trisha grabbing the razor out of my hand and throwing it into the grass. I remember standing there with blood dripping all over the floor. Then someone said we had to go to the hospital.

That's when I started crying. I begged them not to take me. I literally begged—I screamed and wouldn't walk. Tears, more tears than I ever knew I could cry, poured from my swollen eyes.

I remember Trisha pulling me to the car while Jesse went to get a towel, and I remember crying to her, "Have I lost you? Have I lost you?"

I kept repeating that through sobs until she said, "I don't know," which made me even more hysterical.

About that time, Sam and his friend walked up the sidewalk, unsure of what was going on. I think Trisha told them I had gotten sick and we had to go to the hospital. The whole way there, I cried and pleaded with them to leave me alone, take me back to the apartment, that I would be fine, that the cuts were not that bad.

I remember Jesse and Trisha trying to come up with some explanation in case the police or some authority got involved.

I did not know my life was literally bleeding out of me.

We got to the hospital, a lot of which is a blur. It was really bright in there and it hurt my eyes. Jesse was walking ahead of us to get help and Trisha was walking with me, holding a green kitchen towel over my wrist.

Someone told someone else I had cut myself.

I remember a woman in the ER, taking my arm and opening the towel up and saying, "You've done it this time."

They took me to a bed. I don't know the order of things that happened. I don't even know all of what happened there. There were a lot of people at first, asking questions, making judgments, a doctor who wasn't very nice. I lay there for a long time, crying hysterically. Still asking Trisha if she was still going to be my friend. She kept telling me I had to fix myself first, then we'd discuss other things, but I couldn't stand the thought of that. It was like all I could focus on was Trisha, otherwise, I don't know what would have happened to me…if I hadn't had somewhere to focus all the new emotions that had taken over. Fear. Sorrow. Fear. I hadn't even begun to think about what the next few hours would bring; a phone call home to Mom, a 10-hour road trip back to Pennsylvania, a lot of unanswered questions and an uncertain future.

We were there in that room for nearly seven hours. The hospitals computers were down, there were other patients to take care of, the person taking care of me was an intern practicing stitching.

First, I was "assessed." Basically, they put me in an ER bed with a towel wrapped around my arm with several people talking at once, asking questions, giving orders.

One doctor got the bare bones of the story and said it would have easier for me to call Trisha a bitch and leave it at that, rather than cut myself.

She couldn't understand. Probably, she didn't want to.

I don't remember what else happened during that time, other than I cried continuously.

Later, though I don't know how much later, a man came in; the hospital behavioral health something or other. He stood at the foot of my bed with his little clip board, asking questions, most of which I don't remember answering.

I know that once again, I came incredibly close to getting myself thrown in the psych ward. What saved me is the fact that Dr. D. had already prescribed me an anti-depressant that I would be starting when I got home. Another thing is that Trisha was driving me home and would deliver me right to my front door where my mother would be waiting.

I wasn't getting out of it this time.

Much later, someone came in to clean the cuts, which was the most physically painful part. It took a really long time, and when he was done, I laid there for another hour or so with my arm hanging off the bed.

At one point, Sam wanted to come back and see me. When he got there, he took my hand, held it tight and looked at the cuts.

With tears in his eyes, he asked me why.

All I could say was that I was sick.

Later, a doctor came in with the intern. By this point, I was exhausted, so I don't remember much about that either. Just that the doctor told the kid he could do it and then he left.

The young Indian doctor-to-be began his work, one small stitch at a time. He'd maybe gotten five to ten done before the mean doctor came back and said he should do some other kind of stitch that would take less time. She showed him a few, then left him to it again.

Trisha and I both drifted in and out of sleep. I occasionally cried more and tried to get Trisha to talk to me, which she did, but not because she wanted to. I think she did it just to keep me calm.

When he was finally done again, I laid there for hours. Just hours. Soon, Trisha started badgering every doctor, nurse or orderly who walked by. They all said the same thing: "You can't go until we get you processed, and our computers are down."

It was a long, long few hours until we were finally discharged.

We got in Jesse's car and drove back to their apartment. Trisha lay down in my bed with me, but did not touch me or comfort me in any way.

It was too short before we were up again and I dropped to another floor of hell.

Jesse and Sam were still sleeping when Trisha started making phone calls, one to her mother and one to my mother. She went out on the deck and wouldn't let me hear the conversation, so I still don't know what was said between them.

I crawled into bed beside Jesse and woke her up. I know that I apologized and asked her what I could do to make it up to her. She said, "Just get better." If I only could have promised that to her—to anyone at that point.

It was just a little later that Trisha and I were packing up in the car getting ready to head back to Pennsylvania. We kept walking by dried pools of blood all over the staircase, which Trisha tried to clean up with spot remover and a paper towel.

When we pulled out, I waved goodbye and wondered if things would ever be the same between the four of us. How could I ever make things better?

It was a long ride home, for sure. Nearly 10 hours in a car with the best friend whose heart I broke. Ten hours of wondering about the future and what was going to happen when I got home.

What was my mother going to do? Say? How was she going to treat me? Could she still love me after we talked? Could anyone love me after this?

Trisha and I did talk about things, though I don't remember much of the conversation.

We stopped once to get some lunch and while she went in the

store, I called my mother. I remember tears and wobbly voices. I remember her telling me we would get through this, and yes, that she loved me.

She still loved me.

She said she'd meet me at my apartment, and we hung up.

Trisha stayed with me until Mom came. I answered the door, looked at her, she looked at me, I said, "I'm sorry, Mom," and we held on to each other for a few minutes.

I took her into the living room, where she launched right in with the questions. Right away she asked if I knew why I did it. Then she asked if it had anything to do with my father.

I tried to explain about the cutting, why I did it, and its benefits.

She handled it all really well. At least in front of me. I know she was dying inside. I know she probably cried in the shower where I couldn't hear her. Who knows what she was saying to her husband on the phone. Although I got pretty tired of all the questions, she was an angel to me. She really listened and really tried to understand—something I knew she could not.

She reminded me to shower, gave me my medicine, forced me to eat and told me it was okay to sleep.

She listened to my fears about my friends. She agreed she wouldn't when I asked her not to tell my brother or call my father. When I hadn't heard from Trisha, I cried until she let me leave and go to her. When I told her I was ready to be by myself, she left. Even though after she did, I cried even more and wished she had come back.

The only time she broke down in front of me was the day I took the gauze off my wrist to clean it, and she saw the black stitches...she saw what I'd done to myself.

It was horrible and painful to be hugging her and feel her body shake with sobs that I created. It was almost more than I could stand, yet I had to. So did she.

At the time, I of course thought the stitches were cool. They looked how I wanted them to look—thought they should look. They looked how I felt on the inside, and I wished my whole body could be

139

covered in those stitches, have those deep cuts underneath. Sometimes, I still do wish for that. I loved the way they bubbled when I poured peroxide on them, and I wished I could cut them open and rip the stitches out. I wanted to start the process all over again.

It was hard not to, just like it's hard not to reach for that cigarette or hard to keep your fingernails out of your mouth.

I spend a lot of time thinking about cutting, more than people might think I do, even after all this time. I can go for quite some time without thinking about, without longing for it and wishing I had it back again. Then there are weeks, even months at a time when I just obsess over it. I can't stop thinking about it and fantasizing about it. That's the time I usually write a few poems about it, hoping they'll be my fix. It feels good to write it all out, if I can't bleed it all out. It helps, but it's just not the same. Nothing could be, of course.

When I do bring the subject up with someone, usually Tonya, she marvels that I still think of it as much as I do. She wonders why I'm not past it; I wonder that myself. After the long months without it, it's gotten easier, but it still has power over me, still holds me hostage to that power. Usually I would like that, if I were still cutting, of course. But without the cutting, it really is like being held captive by something you hate.

I hate the fact that I write so much about blood and cutting skin. I like my poetry, I'm glad I can write, but that's not the kind of thing that gets you recognized in the world of poetry. It bothers me that the need to write about blood is so strong, I can hardly breathe until I scribble something down about it and finish it later. It bothers me that it still happens and happens so often.

To be cliché, I keep trying to break the chains. I'm not afraid to, it's just that they seem to be made of rubber. They stretch almost to the breaking point, then snap back and hold tight at a moment's notice. Sometimes I don't think it's fair. Sometimes I feel like I've done all the work I can do with this, that I've done more than my part in getting better. So, why do I still have to feel the way I do, how come I still have to struggle so much? Why do I have to be haunted by it so much, and when will it stop?

May 3

I think I wrote before that I was realizing the ugliness of my scars. That's only half true, I guess.

Sometimes I hate them because they remind me of my sins, that night and how much I hurt the people I love the most. It's a horrible thing. Terrible to try and get over the things I've done. The scars help me from getting on with and living life.

I know that my loved ones look at my wrist too. They try to be slick about it, but I'm not dumb.

I see it and can tell. They have a right to look—I know they are curious. But it makes me uncomfortable. And sad. And a little irritated.

When Trisha runs her fingers over the scars, I get mixed emotions. I appreciate that she can touch them and try to heal them up—and I appreciate that she can do that and not get upset all over again. At least outwardly.

I still feel horrible because I don't want to go back there ever, and I don't want her to have to go there either. Even though I took us all there in the first place.

So, it's not fair, really, that I wish everyone could let it go (even though mostly they have, at least with me).

These scars remind everyone of what I did and who I hurt and how. I hate that.

But part of me still looks at the scars and believes they are deserved and cool-looking.

I think that's really wrong, simply because it's such habitual thinking. It's been years, and as they say, old habits die really hard.

So, I don't beat myself up too hard about that.

I think I'm doing really well with everything, considering.

It's all always in the back of my mind. But I'm learning how to not ignore it or let it eat at me, but put it all in perspective, then move on.

As I told everyone, I'm moving on, and they can come with more or not.

Lucky enough for me, they have. At least outwardly. Who the hell knows what's going on in their heads or what they say to everyone else...I would love to read minds.

May 16

I still wonder what I will ever do with these.

They won't mean much to anyone, except maybe a significant other. I'm not sure I'd want my kids (if I have any) reading them.

I don't even want to read them sometimes. And there are so many. So many complaints and dumb thoughts and rantings and ravings…Mean things about other people. Things about myself I'm embarrassed about.

Maybe I should burn these all. Get rid of the evidence. I would cry, though. I really would. They are such a part of me. They are me, really.

May 20

I think I'm going to drop back down to one pill a day. I am not really noticing much difference between one and two. And that's a lot of money to be throwing away if it's not needed. I'm noticing a lot of dizziness these days….I would imagine because of the medicine. Tiredness all of the time…

It's been 10 weeks and 2 days since that terrible night in Virginia…It seems so weird. Like really long ago. Sometimes like a dream. And everything afterward. Talking to Mom, restarting my friendships and love. Beginning to realize I can do just fine without cutting….Realizing blood can be an infatuation, but I don't have to take it to the extreme. I don't have to hurt myself. Other people can do it for me!

But seriously, we get hurt enough. And the hiding, the lying, band-aids and scars….are not worth it.

Slowly but surely, we're getting there. Weirdly enough, I don't really have the urge to cut much anymore—unless I see blood somewhere else, or really get my feelings hurt.

At the same time, the meds help that whole feelings/emotional thing, as I've mentioned.

So, it gets pretty confusing sometimes.

Balancing between old thoughts, feelings and habits with new emotions and standards and expectations.

I have an evaluation tonight with a new doctor. I'm a little nervous. We don't know each other, and I'm uncomfortable answering questions to begin with….add on hard, honest, candid questions, and what will I do then?

I don't even know where to start with everything There were things that took me weeks to tell Mary and I only have a few with this lady. Which is good for my checkbook, but not good for me personally.

But at the same time, I'm ready to be "fixed."

I want to do this and get everyone off my back. Do this and be done—know I'm really not going to cut again. Do this and go to Mary once a month or whatever just to keep in balance.

Do this and be done.

So, I'm nervous to start over and start again. But I don't have a choice right now.

May 22

What a night. I look back at how insouciant I was toward starting with Mary. And how different I was last night. It was such a hard thing. I was already so nervous.

And she's very nice—or seems that way.

Different than Mary, though. She seems sensitive and understanding…but not as much as Mary, I guess.

She first made me cry when she asked me if I planned on teaching [my sister] how to cut herself when she's older. I teared up then and said no; then she asked me if that was a reality check for me—and I cried some more. Then I cried more when I told her about Trisha and Amy and my Jenny. And more when I just glossed over some of the things about my father.

It was strange because in all the time I saw Mary, I never cried at all. Then, 15 minutes with this new lady, I'm a faucet. Go figure.

Her room is like a living room—more so than an office or anything. Comfy couches, fish tank, glass table with a candle burning on it. I'm sure I could get really comfortable there.

Dr. Deb is probably in her late 30s. Blonde hair, blue eyes. Tall, thin. Pretty once I raised my eyes and really looked at her. Can have a gentle voice. Probably wished I were more of a talker.

At the end of the session, I went to shake her hand just as she reached out to give me a hug. She asked if I gave hugs. Ha! I smiled and said, "Yes, I do." It was nice and a bit comforting to be wrapped in her arms. This woman who holds parts of my life in her hands.

But as soon as I left, I started crying again. I just don't get it. I don't understand why I was so scared. Why I'm still so scared.

The whole thing really freaked me out, quite honestly. And yet, I'm sort of anxious to go back and see what happens next.

This is my chance, really. I started fresh, and I haven't held anything back from her, like I did Mary. And I know it's because I have to. Or what a huge waste of time, money and energy.

I think I enjoy the one on one time. Where nobody interrupts me or talks over me. Where it's just about me and her and learning how to live—through everything.

Remembering, hurting, yes. Closing my eyes to the pain and hurt. A hurt so bad that sometimes I'm not sure I can feel anything else ever again.

A kind of helplessness, even though I'm sitting there, doing part of my part in "recovering." Like everything I'm feeling is so big, so overwhelming…Like I'm so small in the universe that is simply Dr. Deb's room.

A kind of loneliness there. Just me and her, and I wish I had Trisha or Jenny or Amy there to hold my hand, or stroke my hair and brush away my tears. That's unfair. But I feel so alone without them. I feel okay with just her….but still alone and helpless. Even though I'm not.

And having any of my friends there…how much would it really help? How could they ever understand any of it? Always on the outside, looking in—still separated by experience, a wall of unknown.

No idea the ocean of emotion ebbing and tiding inside these pounds of bone, skin, organs, blood.

It's incredible. Amazing, really. That so much can happen inside one little person so often and so strongly.

No one else can fully understand. But then—no one is leading me anymore....simply holding my hand along the way for me to squeeze any time I need to.

After all, you can't be saved by anybody but yourself.

Which I believe to be true....but I'm so damn thankful for the angels along the way.

May 23

I so want to write a book. A collection of my journal entries on this whole thing....the entire journey. Put together all of this from start to never-ending finish...if that makes sense.

Because I want to help others like me. Not in a text-book psychiatrist way, but in my way. A very true, real, candid way. A way others like me can really relate to and understand. They can read that they can make it...if they really want to...It's hard, at times horrible, scary, but still an option.

I can keep myself entertained with all my own entries. And Jenny always says I'm a good writer and could help others. Amy says that too...and it makes me feel good—really good.

And how awesome would it be to have a real book about a real thing...and help real people. The more I think about it, the more excited I get about it. How cool.

I've done some surfing on the internet about cutting and such....and most of it is doctor stuff. A few short tales from self-harmer's, but nothing too exciting or detailed, or complete. Nothing really touching. Maybe I'm not looking hard enough. But it would be cool to write a book for others to read and relate to.

Best-seller. People talking. I'll have done something with my life.

I should get started on that...Seriously. I could include my poetry. Hmm. Not a bad idea. That means I'll have three books in the works.

May 27

In going through my old journals, I'm sometimes amazed by some of the things I've written. Like, some of the things are really good! Inspiring, sort of. But I'm impressed with the way the words flow together and are interesting. I'm so anxious to get started.

I do hope, however, that it doesn't end up like my two other "novels." Forgotten and frustrated. But I'm not sure about that. I think this one is different....

I really want to finish—to publish—to tell my story and to help others like me. Or anyone just wanting to read a true story of dark to light—trial to triumph. It's exciting.

Now I have a purpose for most of the newer ones [journals]. And that's cool.

June 3

Today my mom is 49. Holy cow! I was thinking today how lucky I am to have the relationship we do.

I was shopping today in the Dollar Tree...and I stopped in front of the tools section. Cutting tools and razors.

It seemed so long since I'd bought a razor...or even held one. Like a lifetime ago.

I just stared at them—the different colors and sharp points on each corner.

It was like a montage of scenes going through my head—then a montage of blood, cutting, red water in the shower, soaked band-aids, tears....

It was weird.

And for a moment, I longed for how it used to be...but just a fleeting moment. Because I still miss it sometimes.

Maybe not sometimes or at all. If it makes sense. I just miss it. But at the same time....I don't.

It was like the cutting was a strong chain keeping me captive in a dark hole of secrets and hiding and shame. But I'm not chained down anymore, and I really enjoy it...the newish freedom.

There are things still hurting and holding me down...but nothing as much as cutting was. And it's really an awesome feeling.

I am relieved that it's not a part of my present and future anymore. Regardless of the scars that remind me of the past, I know it's the past.

And still I work with Dr. Deb, pushing on to make it all the past. I really like her. I like the way she relates relevant things to how I should feel and such. Because they all make sense and I can see that.

Sometimes I get unnerved by the way she looks at me....like she's waiting for me to say something...but I don't know what, and then I get uncomfortable and start smiling. Which makes the situation worse.

But she's very straight forward, very sincere.

She's the kind of person whose head I'd like to get into while I'm talking. She's the kind of person you feel God directs you to...especially after everything I'd gone through to set up an appointment with her. Or any psychologist.

There must be a reason it's her I'm with now.

I have to admit, I'm not sure of her agenda...She just asks some basic questions every now and then...tells of couple stories and then it's time to go. I just feel there is so much more to me and all of this...

The thing that cracks me up—I'm only scheduled for a series of about 9 sessions, 30 minutes each. Apparently after that, I'm supposed to be cured.

Mom and I laugh about that all the time. It is rather funny. Healed. Cured. Just like that.

It worries me a bit. I just started with Dr. Deb, and while I want to be done with counseling, I don't want to be done before I'm really ready. And I'm sort of afraid Dr. Deb will do that to me....just when I'm starting to really work through some things.

But I guess we'll see.

At any rate—I am certain I'm making some more progress with Dr. Deb than Mary. And that's nothing bad against Mary. That's just how it is.

I think it's funny to look back at some of my old journals—which I'm doing now for the "novel" I'm writing and in which *this* very entry will be included; weird—and seeing how far I've come. When I could never really see it before.

It's almost embarrassing, really. Some of the things I wrote and felt...but all of this what makes me human, I suppose. As embarrassing as that is.

June 6

It's hard to explain how I feel right now.

I'm really tired. My stomach feels pukey. My head feels dizzy—but I'm very alert. I'm very....emotional too.

Like, my insides...if one could see them....it would look a lot like a tornado ripping through farm land. All my emotions, feelings are like the trees and homes, cars and animals flying through the air. It's busy inside me, but I can't figure out why.

I don't think it's the meds. I am experimenting, though. Last week I only took one pill each day. This week, it's 2 every day. I'm looking for any differences....are 2 better than 1?

Is it weird that I can't say for certain? So, does that mean there isn't any difference?

Does that mean I'm not as messed up as we all thought?

Sometimes I get a weird feeling—like I'm so small inside something so big. A statue stuck inside a snow globe that someone is always shaking up.

Like there is so much out there in the world—I want to see so much...but I think I put on my rose-colored glasses a lot. I think about that sometimes.

I know how much bad stuff is going on in the world—the US, this state, this town.

I know it. Feel it. But as easily as I can see it all, I can turn it off. Ignore my mind and focus on my life and family and friends. I think that's wrong sometimes.

But then...I think if I don't turn it off, I'll go crazy thinking about it all and being helpless. And then, I'd be missing out on what I have and hold dear.

But then that makes me selfish.

It's a catch 22. I hate catch 22s. What exactly is a catch 22? Who came up with that?

I know that sooner or later I'm going to have to write about "that night."

It seems easy to ignore. But at the same time, I can never really ignore it. More importantly, I've written so much leading up to it—and so much after it.

There's a large part missing right now.

But there! Right now, I just had a flashback of it all, and it hurt so bad. I even teared up. Can I handle any of it now? I just don't know.

It hurts so much. Everything hurts so much. I'm so tired of hurting.

I'm doing fine, I know that. I'm well on my way…but it still hurts. Sometimes I can forget or ignore…numb myself to it.

I guess that's partly because I'm used to it by now.

And sometimes I want to rip myself open and let it all fly out and away from me.

I imagine it pretty poetic, almost.

Standing on some sort of cliff, clouds and tiny but bright rainbows dotting a light blue sky.

I breathe in deeply and as I exhale slowly, my rib cage opens up, the tornado inside me spins right out of my chest….

It breaks into pieces in the wind—all those emotions break into pieces and turn into bright butterflies.

They fly to the clouds and the rainbows, taking it all with them….I breathe in again, my chest closes itself up. And I'm free.

Huh. Not bad. Reminds me a little of a Skittles commercial, though.

June 6; an email from Amy after reading the introduction for this book:

You have to follow this through. It is my belief that we all have a purpose in life—and sometimes God doesn't always make it real clear up front what it should be. You summed it up beautifully….why it takes the doctors—and counselors to explain the "backbone" of the disease—it takes a real person…someone who has lived it…is living and will live it to relate it to the people who will benefit from the knowledge. You are on the way to something very great….stay on the path…and enjoy the journey…and remember….there will always be your "coalition" cheering you on!

Love ya,

Amy

June 10

I guess all it really takes sometimes is just one moment of clarity. I know that I've had a few in my life. What's amazing is that sometimes, they still come. Either of my own accord or with some help.

Today I had some help from, who else, Dr Deb, Miracle-worker. I think I've said this before (wrote, sorry). But she's very good at what she does. She has a way of making her voice heard so that even the toughest barriers and doors I've constructed fall to her words.

She says I'm amazing...but I find her completely amazing and fascinating.

I wonder how she, and others like her, can do it. I thought that as she said goodbye to me and welcomed her next client, who happened to be a nun.

It's a wonder these people can go from on person's sob story to another, and another. All day long. Then go home and be normal. That's as amazing as us on the other side going through what we do and being able to carry on. What strength Dr. Deb and Mary must have.

I think one of the things I do miss about Mary is her time. Sessions were always an hour, sometimes more—there was always time to chat, talk, get to know each other. It bothers me that that's missing now.

Because I'm just a curious person to begin with—I want to know about people, especially people who know so much about me. I don't think Dr. Deb is as open as Mary. And that's fine, just different.

And she does fascinate me, so I want to know everything about her.

I wish I could remember everything she said to me today...because it did strike some chords. It did make sense. It empowered me and made me think...she's got to be right.

While she spoke, I envisioned myself morphing. A big zipper down my middle—it's pulled and a new me steps out. The same me, but a me with no preconceived notions, no fallible opinions of myself.

Nothing inside but what is supposed to be there—my bones, blood, fiber, tissue...my "essence." And essence, I must admit, that I hope reaches people now.

I want people to see that of me—and essence is just such a beautiful word. I want to be beautiful.

If I am, maybe it's time to let myself see that. Scars and all.

I'm not supposed to take anything personally...which I still think is rather difficult. But she's right, my Dr. Deb.

As far as the whole "good enough" thing....She's probably right about that too.

She said cutting myself to get rid of the bad is futile because there's nothing bad in me. She says I am good. I am pure. When I look at her, into her eyes, as she tells me that, I have to believe her. If only for a few moments...those moments will eventually take me to the sky as they build on one another.

It is an exciting time, I guess. My life as a victim [of self-mutilation] is about to come to an end. Now life as a survivor begins.

Although I'm not too fond of either term.

I'm just me—an "amazing" person with fire and fight left in her. An essence.

It's not that I feel sorry for myself. I just feel apart. And what I discover along the re-building process is like the glue holding each piece of me together. It's pretty strong glue too.

I've learned—though I still sometimes wish I could and want to cut, I don't have to. In the long run, it accomplishes nothing; it only brought more bad things and pain.

I've learned—I am and will be responsible from now on what I do to myself. As a direct result of what I've learned from the above statement.

There are a lot of things in my life I am not responsible for. I don't want to hold myself responsible for the cutting.

Circumstances larger than myself precipitated that...and I won't hold myself responsible for that March night either.

As far as I'm concerned, that's rock bottom...a place that cannot be helped. You've got to get there to get out. Nobody hits rock bottom deliberately, including myself.

So, I forgive myself for that night. It was beyond my control.

I forgive myself for my selfishness, for hurting the people I love most.

I forgive myself for putting myself through everything I have.

I forgive myself for being me.

Now it's time to finish gluing. It's time.

Geez. All of that out of one half hour.

Damn. She is good.

Now this is not to say I won't struggle. That I don't have "days" ahead of me. That I don't need help anymore. That would be a ridiculous notion.

I still need that proverbial wind under my wings—from my mom, my friends and Dr. Deb.

It's still scary territory, for sure. And the healing is not complete.

I'm like a giant scab right now. The middle process of healing, but I can still be picked apart and picked off....

July 7

And the more I thought about it, the more mad I got and the more sad for [my brother]. Because I can plan it all out in my head, can see it and even feel the uncomfort. It's so unfair....it has been. But now I'm just so angry about it. And there really isn't anything I can do about any of it. We'll never feel better or get anything back from all those years. We'll never get anything in the future. And there is nothing I can do about it. Except take it and "move on." And that just kills me. Because it's so unfair. And my father gets away with it all. While the rest of us are in the wake of his destruction.

And lately I've been thinking I could let go of him now if not for [my sister]. I love her and it's not her fault. I won't hold anything against her, but the fact remains....she's there. Spoiled, and I'm glad she's getting the things she needs, but there is no reason my brother and I had to see how hard it was for Mom to make sure we had those things too. He's a selfish man. And when Mom said he's pathetic, I have to agree. Even though I have to try really hard to not feel bad about it.

I don't owe him anything. And by God I will find a way to separate him and [my sister]. I will find a way to keep her, but lose him.

And not feel guilty about it.

I'm just so tired of it all. And would love for it to be over. For myself and for my brother because he's been through enough too. And he deserves to feel happy and leave our father behind, as well.

But I feel extra bad for him now because Mom told him about me. I wanted her to, but I didn't. And that all hurt him too. I am so tired of hurting people with all of this—I was hoping it would be over. But I forgot about my brother. So now I feel guilty that he feels guilty— he told Mom he wished he'd been a better brother so I would have had someone to talk to. And that killed me. Because even though my counselors told me I could be angry at both of them, I have never been. I couldn't and wouldn't. But I also can't stop them from feeling guilty and sad about it—even though I don't want them to.

***

There are so many things that come into play when you're recovering from something. There are reasons that you tell yourself why you should recover. There are reasons you make up for why you shouldn't.

One of the strongest things that keeps someone like me on the proverbial wagon is accountability. I'm lucky enough to have family and friends who care about me a whole lot. And I, in return, care about them a great deal. Care about what they think and feel and everything about them. As previously mentioned, I hate hurting people and already had so deeply with all of this. So after Hospital Night, when I swore I was done cutting, I had to be, whether I was ready or not for quitting cold turkey.

I couldn't keep doing this to the people I loved. I couldn't put them through that or the horror if something happened, and I got out of control one night and ended up dead. I couldn't stand the thought of losing my friends if they couldn't deal with me and the cutting anymore. Shortly after the stitches, Trisha threatened me with that, and I knew others would have to follow suit. My mother threatened to send me to a psychiatric hospital in Pittsburgh if I cut again. And who knew what would happen with my job, my career?

So day by day, month by month, whenever I wanted to cut, I stopped to think about what it would do to someone else...even just that one last time I always wanted. It would ruin all the trust I was starting to build back up with everyone. I would ruin confidence; in myself and the confidence of others. I would be a disappointment to myself and others. Every day I didn't cut was a victory, a miracle at times. I wanted to be victorious. I wanted to be a miracle, even. I wanted to succeed at this and prove everyone wrong who thought I'd backslide and give in and never make it. And I was putting my loved ones ahead of myself, using them as my strength to get through.

Someone once told me I needed to do this for myself, nobody else. But sometimes, I'm not sure that's an option. After all, I was cutting myself. Why would I stop for myself? All this time later, though, I realize it was for me, even if only partly, and even though I didn't know it at the time.

July 8
And my Dr. Deb verified that for me today...she basically said we are all adults who feel. But what they feel now isn't really because of me, but rather Dad, when it comes down to it.

She says I'm not responsible for their feelings or my dad's, as I walk down the path.

It's still really hard, though, because I'm just that kind of person. I don't like to hurt anyone or feel bad because I think I did.

She reminded me that I don't owe him anything and shouldn't worry about his feelings since he doesn't worry about mine. She said I should tell him how I feel if the opportunity comes up because, really, who cares. He just brings me down—and it's true. I feel that I'm at the point where I could do that....if not for [my sister].

The last page of this never-ending journal. A bit under a year to finish it.

I feel like I skipped so many important things in here—during this time in my life...but oh well.

I've learned so much along the way—and those words of lessons are written deeply on my heart...and that's good enough for me.

July 8, 2003, 8:32 p.m.

July 10, 2003

Lighthouses are so amazing....just looking at one makes me feel strong. They are so powerful, so stoic no matter what comes their way. And though they may crumble and fall from constant ebbs and tides, they don't go easily.

That's another reason I want to be a lighthouse...or maybe at least be thought of as similar.

But I've realized...lighthouses may be out on islands alone or hanging onto shore by a stone, still so strong and reliable...but they aren't alone. They can't do their job alone all the time...even the brightest need help from others to keep so many safe. Otherwise there wouldn't be so many lighthouses.

We can all be as strong, non-bending and bright as light from Heaven. We can be symbols of hope and beauty and safety...but we all still need to see all that in ourselves.

And we all need others to see it too...point it out to us.

What's most important...is to realize no matter how much we want to be a lighthouse, we can't do it alone.

I still need her (Amy) to talk to in the newsroom in the mornings and feel that she really cares and isn't just trying to make conversation the way she would with anyone else. I need her to call me on the phone and share stupid stories with. I need her to hold my hand every now and then just because that's what friends do. And hold my hand when I wake up from a nightmare, when I'm scared or lonely, sad or confused. When I'm dealing with my dad and when I want to cut.

I need her to smile at me and make me laugh. I need her to just be my friend.

July 16

It's a few days after the visit with my dad…and I still feel the same. A million different things at once. Mostly confusion. Sadness. It was so hard to watch them drive away with [my sister] in her car seat, her little head looking at me through the window.

July 25

The visit was a mix of everything. I was so nervous. I hadn't seen any of them in more than a year. Just seen [my sister] in pictures and heard my dad on the phone. I don't "know" any of them—haven't for years. Wow. A decade now…more than, actually. And all of those years have just been filled with pain and confusion. I'm never exactly thrilled to see my dad.

But thank God for [my sister]. My baby sister. I was so excited to see her, touch her, smell her. She's so beautiful….and sweet. Everything babies are. But this baby is mine. Her smile is like a light bulb. And her little baby voice is just so sweet. She had me in constant fits of laughter….and I wish it were just me and her. Because I was still uncomfortable with Dad and [his wife].

I just kept reminding myself that the visit was for [my sister]. She's all I care about. But being who I am, I was worried about keeping everyone else happy. Like [my dad's wife] who wanted to go to the Antique Depot. And Dad who wanted to watch a movie on the "visit" and ended up falling asleep on the floor. I guess a lot of it was just hurtful. I don't know why I was surprised. I guess I was just hoping for different. It's a shame that it's so hard to enjoy spending time with my own family. Especially when I want [my sister] so bad.

And I'm just so tired of all these tug-of-war feelings inside me. Everything I've written about before—guilt, anger, confusion, sadness, overwhelmed, tired…

I have no idea if there will come a time when those all go away, as I wish they would.

But I guess with each day, they kind of all start meshing together…shrinking maybe. And sticking to one small part of my brain. Not running wild throughout the entire thing. I suppose I'll always cry when he leaves. I'll always think of all the hurtful things he brought me.

But I'm hoping I can just think of it all briefly, and then move on.

But it was wonderful to be with my sister. And now it's hard to be apart because I want her with me so badly. It's even harder to think of all I'm missing. I'm constantly thinking of her. But I just can't keep doing what I did at the visit…I don't know how many times I could do that in a year.

So, that's hard to deal with too. It never ends.

August 1

I feel weird tonight—out of sorts. Scared. Feel like crying. Or cutting. Or both. I'm not sure what brought it on. I was fine after work. Went for a run. Felt good then.

Now I have no idea. I haven't felt this way in so long.

I had a quick vision of cutting—it ran like fast forward in my head. And I came pretty close to doing it—well, not all that close. But closer than I would have liked.

Thinking about it made me feel happy…or at least relieved, almost. But scared too, because it's so unpredictable. And I thought maybe I'd be getting over all of that. But it's still there…still there. I guess that's my life. I'll be fighting this always.

I tired to call Amy, but she wasn't home. Jenn has company tonight and Trisha is with her mom. There are others I could call— but I don't feel as though I can talk openly to them. And that's what I probably need. So, I write instead.

Though I long to feel strong arms wrap around me. A soft voice tell me it's okay.

Wow. I don't even feel like I'm here right now. I feel like curling up in a ball or something. For the first time in a long time, I'm afraid. But of what?

This "disease?" Myself? Weakness? The impending night? Which I used to love so much…tonight adds to the fear in my head and heart. It's just a summer night. But it brings tears to my eyes. What is wrong with me?

It's still beautiful, though…the night. I feel like I should do something—but I am still having a hard time. …so instead, I enjoy it's beauty and mystery through my big windows. Wondering what others are doing tonight. Anyone else out there feeling like me…anyone thinking of me? A piece of that sky up there for me…protecting me.

Breathe. Just breathe. This will end…this isn't forever. You are stronger than any of your feelings. You are stronger than your skin and anything that can break it open.

I give in to the tears…I wish I knew why they came. It makes no sense. I feel frozen in this spot—kneeling here against my radiator cover, in front of my windows. Like I'm powerless to move…I'm a little shaky.

If I could just get up…make my way to bed…maybe I'd just fall asleep and wake up me again.

August 3

I find myself unable to sleep tonight. My arms and legs keep twitching, I can't settle down. My mind works overtime. I still want to cut. So badly. I think it would relax me like it used to. Visions run through my mind of cutting myself. Cutting everywhere. I want to cut *whore* into my arm and slash open every other part of me. My legs and arms and stomach and chest. I just want to be covered in blood. I want my nights in the shower back—the water turning red from my own red blood pouring out of me. I should look like the girl from *13 Ghosts*.

I just want to feel that razor in my hand again—such comfort.

But I think Amy is right…and it's 4:30 a.m. and I just called her at work and asked for help…talk me out of it because I don't want to fuck up again….She's right. I've come so far, done so well…I am the strongest person she knows. I've come so far, and if I give in, I will be so mad and disappointed and angry and helpless that I'll have forgotten why it's worth fighting…I will be pissed if I do it.

And I do fear that if I had one last chance, I wouldn't be able to write about it.

Because I'd be dead.

I'm guessing four months—four long months—of not doing it, not dragging that blade through my skin, has built up somewhat. I don't know if I'd be able to stop

So, I visualize in my head instead…run my thumb over the razor's edge. Press it to my left wrist and take satisfaction in the slow, deliberate cut I create across my skin. The blood springs to the surface, builds and breaks, dripping down, running across my skin.

I drive the razor again and again into me, not paying attention to where it strikes. One after another. My skin is so covered I can't see anything but red. I turn my arm over and watch it drip and spatter on the shower floor.

It makes beautiful designs. For now, I am satisfied. I have been hurt and punished. Yet I feel alive and calm and in my place.

Never as good as the real thing…but we'll take it for now.

August 4

Geez. That's all so crazy. When do I get to stop looking back at cutting as so satisfying?

I thought I was doing so well…doing well not thinking about it so much, not longing for it, wishing for it…I hate having that feeling in my stomach…like a rock is in there pulling all my emotions down to the bottom of it…because it's like something isn't right. A huge part of me is missing…and I can't have it back. I'll never make beautiful blood patterns again. Never slap band-aids on my wrist and carry on thinking everything is ok. My visions are like fantasies. They'll never come true.

August 5; an email from Amy during a particularly rough night and morning.

You can get through this!!

One step at a time….take it 30 minutes at a time….

the sun brings a new day with new energy!!

Call me for breakfast!!

August 14

The weirdest thing—I was sweeping out the van the other day and found an old razor blade buried under some stuff. My first instinct was to sweep it up, but just as quickly, I pulled back.

It was weird to have one in my hand again, even though I think about it so often.

I held it, turned it over and over in my hand, ran my thumb along its sharp edge, pressed it to my left wrist. It happened quickly, but I didn't do anything...just held it there, feeling its sharpness and remembering.

I guess I was stronger than I thought I would be if put in that position once more. And I was proud of myself....I guess.

Then I thought, "I was given that 'one more time' I'm always moaning about." I realized I was getting it...but the weird thing? It wasn't satisfying as I'd imagined it would be. Maybe because I couldn't cut. Or maybe because I really am moving on...I'm just not sure.

I didn't really feel any of the old comfort. It just felt familiar. I do hope I can remember that next time I feel like cutting or whatever.

Once I realized I was having my "one more time" I pretty much ended it. I threw the blade out the window while I was driving...which I later felt guilty about for two reasons. Littering, for one and I had a huge fear that someone would run over it and blow their tire out and cause a huge crash and it would be all my fault.

But so far, none of that has happened. Every time I drive by Exit 23, I think of the whole situation and incident.

It was just weird. But interesting. A learning experience.

And something else I recently discovered...well, technically, I re-discovered jelly bracelets. Which was cool. I sort of missed those things once I saw them again.

Anyway, I hooked two together on each wrist like we used to do back in the day. I discovered that felt cool on my wrists. That I liked them there...and then I realized why—it felt like my wrists were bound up with gauze and tape. Like I'd sliced my wrists and they were healing. And weird, but I just love that feeling...I guess because it always went along with cutting—band-aids and stuff...It kind of tricks me into thinking I cut when I didn't.

So, it's a new trick. I'm so tricky.

September 10
Sometimes I feel like I'm not even living my own life...or like I'm not allowed to or something.

It's weird because it's like it never stops. The conversations about me go on behind my back...like I don't even count. And I know everyone talks about everyone...but I can't help but think it's somehow different with my situation. Like I deserve to know what my friends are saying about my life—a big part that I included them in. It's like I'm still exactly how they want to see me....not how I really am anymore. Still. They ask each other about me, but they never ask me. They make up scenarios and tell each other how I must be feeling and what I'm thinking. They decide what I should be doing and to whom and when and how it would make them feel. Doesn't matter what I'm going through or trying to figure out.

They want to take matters into their hands...because I'm not doing it fast enough or well enough.

They think I don't care.

They think think think. But no one ever bothers to ask me what I think about what they think. Or what I think at all. And it hurts.

So, it goes around and I'm a living a life I don't even know about. It makes me tired because, again, I'm that damn hamster again. I keep going around trying to move forward in a good direction, but I can't because every time they talk about me without consulting me or including me, it keeps up the basis of secrecy. Shame. Hiding.

I don't know if that makes any sense at all. I don't know if I could ever make it make sense. I just know it hurts.

And the kicker is, Monday, the 8th was six months since I've cut myself. Six months. I guess it seems like a pretty big deal. Seems more significant than, like, six weeks? I guess I am kind of proud, happy. Accomplished. And I wanted to tell them all—scream it from the roof. But I didn't tell anyone. Not even Trisha. I'm not entirely sure why. It didn't seem important enough—that they would care. It felt like it would just be another passing thing—another conversation nobody wanted to have. Because they're tired of it. Who cares anymore?

So I just kept it to myself. I guess if everyone wants me to "do this for myself" I'll keep it to myself. It's kind of a lonely success. And it doesn't have to be, I know that. I do have wonderful friends…and I know I can go to my mother. But I'm still uncomfortable with that. Sometimes she wants to know too much. Sometimes I can't talk because I don't want to hurt her anymore.

So I'm stuck again. The hamster. Just call me Hammy.

I'm tired just writing and thinking about all of this…

Six months without cutting. Seems long, yet fast. I could read back through so much about how hard it's been. And it has been. Incredibly hard. But I did it. Day by day, hour by hour, scene by scene….I'm still here.

Told you so.

***

That's something else. Not knowing when or how to approach your friends or family to talk about things. Especially once you get into therapy.

For instance, every week, I get the call from my mom.

"Just wanted to see how your appointment went this week."

"Oh, it was fine."

"Well, like, fine how?"

"I mean it wasn't anything special. It was just fine."

"Well, what did you talk about?"

That's the hard thing. The *what did you talk about* question. The inevitable. And when you don't answer in full detail, she gets a little upset, a little hurt. That's happened with Trisha too.

The point is, I go to therapy to talk very openly and freely about things. To a person with no personal involvement with any other part of my life. Dr. Deb doesn't know anyone in my life. She just listens and offers unbiased opinions. I can't hurt her with the things I say…at least personally. I pay her to be confidential with what I say. That's what she's there for. And I can talk to my mom and to Trisha, sure. But there are a lot of things I'm uncomfortable sharing with them. And besides, sometimes an in-depth session with Dr. Deb is enough to make me not want to even think about anything until the next week.

But then, the other side is, sometimes I do want people to ask me things, as you can tell by parts of that last journal entry. Of course, prying and trying to get all the information is a turn-off because it's uncomfortable to be put on the spot like that. And uncomfortable when you don't want to answer. But sometimes, if people come to me, it's like knowing they still care, still want to know how I'm doing. Start out simply, and if I feel like talking, I will.

And yet another side is…just when can you go to someone and talk? I wrote in my journal that my friends might not care about my going six months without cutting. I thought they may be sick of me and all that drama. And I just can't put my heart and mind out there to them when I don't know how they feel about me anymore. I need to know they are still in it, as deeply as I am. But, then again, they may be too shy to come to me and let me know.

It goes around and around. And the bottom line is, communication always needs to be open. Always. And there has to be understanding from everyone. It's so easy to push self-mutilators away. And it's so easy to hurt feelings. So it is a delicate balance, but one that needs to be established somehow.

October 10; an email from Tonya
Rissa,

Thank you for sending me some of your "stuff." That's a cool word that we can thank George Carlin for—I don't know if you've ever heard of his "a place for my stuff" routine, but it humorously reduces the complex meanings of life to a very very simple concept— people and their stuff. Don't let the term fool you — stuff is extremely valuable, meaningful, and in some ways the core of our existence.

Enough philosophy—I'm fighting the urge to say I enjoyed reading
what you wrote—because that isn't accurate—one can't enjoy words
that came from such pain. Instead I will say that I am honored that
you shared it with me and I encourage you to continue to do so.
Hell—I'll buy the book—it hopefully will shed some light (and hope)
on a coping skill that few know much about. Keep writing kiddo—
it just might help all of us.
Love ya,
Ton

Things I've Learned From My Psychologist

1. I *am* a Charlie's Angel
2. I am a Survivor (Just like Destiny's Child sings)
3. I am a Fighter (Like Christina Aguilera sings)
4. I don't have to feel guilty about being human
5. I'm allowed to speak my mind
6. I am worthy of living
7. I have self-worth
8. I have worth
9. I'm allowed to feel
10. I'm allowed to feel the way I feel
11. Don't get stuck in a feeling

Things I've Always Wanted to Do

1. Kick in a door
2. Throw a drink in someone's face
3. Put on a Sumo Wrestler's costume and bounce off of someone else's chest
4. Whip out an ID batch and say "FBI."
5. Whip out a gun from my pants and scream, "FBI, freeze, motherfucker!"
6. Put on all black, skin-tight pleather with guns strapped to all parts

of my body and do the slow-motion movie walk to cool bass-thumping music
7. Learn every country and capital in the world
8. Learn Tujijtsu
9. Meet Oprah
10. Bungi jump
11. Dance the Broadway musical, *42nd Street*

December 28

When I was home over Christmas, I was going through Mom's card baskets, like I always do. I came across the letter Amy wrote to my mother in the weeks after "Hospital Night."

Of course I read it. It's been so long since it happened, and besides….they're out for all to see.

I thought it was nice—very Amy-like.

It killed me to read her paragraph about me being manipulative. That word again. It still has the power to cut me. It's so hurtful to think she either thinks or thought that…and then to have her share that opinion with my mother.

And I guess that perhaps I still don't know what she means by me being manipulative…she never really explained. And she's not a doctor…to be saying that about me in such a way.

It made my heart sink. I don't want my own mother thinking I'm that way…even if it's not the case anymore.

December 29

What else struck me about the letter…she wrote to my mom that she was still concerned and nervous. Of course, that was a long time ago, so maybe she's not anymore. But she also wrote she feared I wasn't strong enough to make it through and do what I needed to do to get better.

She thought I wasn't strong enough.

She thought I was weak.

It's painful when your friends have no faith in you.

I don't recall her, or anyone else, telling me straight up I couldn't do it. I guess I had my doubts whether they believed in me. At the same time, I hoped they did.

And now that I know Amy didn't, I'm hurt.

Even though she had every reason to think I didn't *want* to stop cutting...she didn't think I could.

Again, it hurts.

But...I feel a certain kind of...I don't know, pride? Snottiness? Something between the two that I'm proving her wrong. I am proving them all wrong.

And even myself.

Sure...I used to doubt myself. But that's my right!!

I didn't know if I could make it from day to day without cutting myself...but deep inside, I knew I had to. And that one small feeling kept me going this far...

And when I think about it, I guess I'm not giving Amy enough credit.

If I couldn't completely trust myself, how could she?

Sometimes I'm so confused in my own head. And it makes me so tired.

It's hard to believe that in three months, it'll be one year. One year since I've cut. Put a razor to my skin and sliced...it seems longer than a year. And sometimes it seems like regular time...like a year.

And even thought I *am* so much stronger now, I still find myself feeling split a lot of times.

I'm much happier, but I'm not happy.

I'm much stronger, but I'm not without temptation.

I'm better off without cutting, but I still long for it.

I wonder if I'm doing that to myself. Am I holding myself back still? After all this time?

Is it the only thing I can hold on to about it all, so I do? That's being pretty weak in itself.

Maybe that just takes more time.

December 30
I haven't seen Dr. Deb in three weeks, and I'm starting to feel it.

Something in me doesn't feel right. But I don't know what, and maybe she can help me figure it out. Help me feel better. My emotions are all over the place today...actually, more like in the last few minutes. Isn't that crazy? I was fine and all of the sudden, I can't keep myself in check.

Am I really crazy? Could I finally get that bi-polar diagnosis I've been waiting for?

I'm so sad....for no reason.

I miss Dr. Deb. I miss Mary a lot. I miss Tonya too.

Somehow, my life doesn't seem as full when they aren't in it like I want them to be.

I feel like every possible emotion is slamming into my body at turbo speed—through my skin and into my blood and soul. But the back of me is a brick wall they can't pass through. When they hit, they shatter into pieces. Like glass, their edges are sharp and cut up my insides even more.

I'm full of fragments of sharp emotions, and it hurts so much.

I can't breath....

And I cry because I'm scared and confused and helpless.

And I can't handle what's going on inside of me.

What is? And when will those pieces of emotions finally make me whole?

December 31

I do think New Year's Eve is overrated...this year is no different.

Although, in my own way, I do have hopes and dreams and expectations for the new year.

It's always nice to start fresh, and it's nice to feel like you've got a new start. Even if it's only for one day.

For one day to really hope this is the year of peace.

The year a cure or two come about.

The year human rights apply to everyone.

The year all countries can rebuild from natural disasters and realize we can help each other.

The year everyone accepts God and His son, sent to erase our sins.

Personally—the year I accept who I am and use that person for as much good as I can.

The year I come to terms with my past hurts and use them to my advantage.

A year of less tears.

A year of small successes and triumphs.

And for my family and friends....a year of love, peace and joy.

No tears, no hurts, no sickness or sorrow.

Here's to 2004.

God bless us all.

8:58 p.m.

Green Hills

Over the green hills
The light is brighter—
    A sign that truly
I am on the right path
    To where Jesus waits
    With His angels and saints,
    Ready to lead me home.
I preach His word
And honor His name—
    My promise that faithfully
I am His daughter,
    And I will not fall
    When He does call
To share in His home of glory.
I cry for His death and
Shout He is risen—
    His sign that truly
I am saved
    And will stand
    At God's right hand,
When the Redeemer guides me home.
Over the green hills
The cross stands high—
    Heaven's sign that truly
Peace is mine
    And angel wings wait
    Inside the golden gate,
When Jesus takes me home.

169

I don't think it's any secret that I'm a religious person. I always have been. Especially in high school and college, when I'd go to church every Saturday evening, say the Rosary every Sunday and take Lenten practices to the extreme; fasting, silence and prayer. When I graduated and moved to Pittsburgh, that all kind of waned for some reason. I moved to work on-air and after a few months, probably the most spiritual occurrence that I could have ever hoped to have took place.

I remember it so clearly. I was standing outside of the Hopewell Township Municipal Building and it was around Easter time. It was gray and cloudy. I was waiting for someone to come out and do an interview with me, and I was gazing up at the sky. It was probably a pretty rough day, one of the rougher times in my life in dealing with all of my problems. I was thinking about God and Jesus, and I made a silent plea in my head. I thought something to the effect of, "God, if you're there, please touch me with your love." I know it sounds so stupid, so unreal. But this feeling washed over me, a feeling almost too strange to put into words. It was a feeling of total warmth that spread from the inside out, over my whole body. My eyes filled up with tears, but they were tears of joy and wonderment. I knew God was answering me at that time, a person at just about rock bottom. He knew I needed Him and His comfort. That was the best feeling, and one I found myself relying on as I neared the very bottom. Even now, I turn to that day and God's promises.

What I still had to learn was that I was made in God's image, and He designed each and every thing about me, for me, for Him. Mary and Dr. Deb spent a lot of time talking about that with me, preparing me for some pretty amazing statements.

Such as, "Your body is temple of God," and "You're actually showing God disrespect by mutilating your body." At first, I didn't quite believe that. After all, I didn't think I was worth anything, let alone the power and glory of God. In fact, I thought I was showing God how sorry I was that I couldn't measure up by cutting up myself. And besides, some religions are based on the ideas of scaring and flagellation.

My doctors continued to beat the truth about God and my body into my head, until it started to make sense to me, started to seem true.

Like not wanting to let down my doctors, family and friends, I certainly didn't want to let God down either. I didn't want Him disappointed in me, thinking I was wasting the gift of life He had given to me, wasting His love for me.

That love was always there, I just had to trust it enough to accept it.

March 8, 2004

What a day…what a year that has culminated to this day. 365 days. 12 months. One year.

One year since I last cut myself. I don't even know what to write, really. I'm feeling so many things that are all screaming for attention that I can't concentrate on any of them and end up trying to ignore them all.

I knew this day was coming for a few weeks. I've smiled a few times in thinking of my progress and accomplishments. Other times I've felt nothing.

I don't know how to interpret that. I don't even know if I am really feeling nothing or if I just don't want to feel.

Sometimes it seems so long ago that I was in the hospital…like more than a year, more like a lifetime. Fuzzy and numb if I don't let it all in, don't examine any of it.

But it's too damn clear other times—almost like it's all happening inside of me, all over again.

Sometimes it's like waking up and being in the same day over and over.

I know I have come a long way. To go a year when I didn't know I could go one day…to fight such a huge battle between two of me…and have the right one win.

Sometimes, I look at my scars now, and I know that cutting again could never be or feel the same. Fill whatever void, be the needed drug.

It's like—I still miss it (though not as much as earlier in the battle) but don't want it anymore.

Like an old relationship.

I think it's crazily fitting that I finally got to watch *Thirteen* today. It was an amazing work of art—portrayal of real life. For so many young girls. It was really powerful and a lot of it did speak to this fragile heart of mine.

Especially the cutting, of course.

Then the scene where the mother finds out about the drugs…and her cutting. It was just amazing. The daughter sill hating, but having to give in. The mother totally floored by the stranger she thought she knew, but overcome by love for her baby, her daughter. Her own blood and body. That connection wasn't severed, no matter what had happened. That little girl still needed her mother even after all the adult things she did.

It was just amazing—and when I think about it, it makes me pretty emotional, even hours after I watched the movie.

I can't explain it completely. The images just pound on me. I feel helpless, even though the character isn't me, and even though she was a *real* person and is better.

So many out there aren't. They don't even know they can be better….Hell, *I* hurt over it, still sometimes.

I believe Dr. Deb when she tells me this is all just a small part of me. It doesn't have to be anything else. What other people need to understand—no, it doesn't. And it won't be, the more support and help cutters (or any self-mutilator) gets. It simply takes time for the black hole to lose power, shrink away into a freckle on skin, a cell, a drop of blood pulsing through veins.

I suppose cutters need to understand that too…nothing worth fighting for comes easily.

And…it's taken me this long…

But I'm worth fighting for.

That girl in the movie was worth fighting for.

And so am I.

And so are all of the others out there like me.

It can be done.

My scars have become part of me....I put them there for a reason once.

Sometimes I may choose to cover them up.

Sometimes I may choose to keep them visible...as a symbol, a reminder to myself and everyone else of the struggle and battle that I won.

I'm stitched in more ways than one.

Standing

How am I still standing when I should have laid down so long ago?
What is it that keeps me from falling under the weight of my own mind?
I've been brought to my knees, but something won't let me be pushed down farther.
Something won't let me die.
Though my breathing is choked with imperfection, and my skin heavy with sadness
I'm still alive.
And even if I have to crawl, I'm still standing.

I don't even feel like I'm here, nothing seems real.
My frame isn't holding my soul up,
But it must be because my feet are touching the ground.
And I must be alive because I'm not lying down.
Self-deprecation flows with my blood, and a wall of self-loathing encircles my heart,
But I'm not broken, still I carry on.
And even if I don't know it, I'm still standing.

I feel like I should die, because I don't deserve to live,
I won't let myself feel anything else.
But what is it that won't let me surrender completely?

Something won't let me die.

I am stitched in more ways than one. I know that, and I think the people around me know that. I'm not the same person I once was.

Even as I write these final pages, I know that those other girls are in my past, though they'll always be a part of me. Sometimes I'm thankful for that, sometimes it's a curse.

I don't know if I'll live out the rest of my life dreaming about blood, reminiscing about the "good old days" when I could cut myself. I don't know if I'll always have to write about blood and cutting or always feel like I'm dying inside. I don't have all of the answers. I don't know what my future holds or where I'll end up.

I do know that I'm strong enough now to deal with whatever happens. It's still not the easiest thing for me to do, but I know how to reach out for help and where to find it. I know that I'm doing the best I can, and that best is truly getting me somewhere.

I hope these journalings of mine brought this issue into a brighter light for everyone. It deserves that. It's a legitimate problem that affects so many people in so many ways. I got tired of keeping it a secret. I don't want anyone else to be in that trap either.

I pray I can show just one person who cuts that things can turn out all right.

There is hope.

It is work and it hurts like hell.

But it can be done.

I know. Because I did it

May 2004

References and Further Reading

Self-mutilation and self-harm are issues that are real and dangerous and need to be addressed and corrected as soon as possible for the welfare and safety of the person. If you know anyone who needs help, don't hesitate to get it for them. If you are a self-mutilator and need help, don't wait—you are important.

The following are just a small sample of the reading material out there. There is a large selection of books, both fiction and non about this topic. There are also thousands of websites that cover this issue with first-hand accounts, professional opinions and advice, threads and chat rooms.

1 (800) DONTCUT (366-8288)
www.palace.net/~llama/psych/injury.html
www.healthatoz.com/healthatoz/Atoz/ency/self-mutilation.html

Favazza, A.R., (1996) Bodies Under Siege: Self-Mutilation and Body Modification in Culture and Psychiatry. Baltimore, MD: The Johns Hopkins University Press.

Kettlewell, Caroline (2000) Skin Game: A Memoir. St. Martin's Press

Levenkron, Steven, (1998) Cutting: Understanding and Overcoming Self-Mutilation.
Norton, W.W. & Company, Inc.

Levenkron, Steven (1999) Cutting: Norton, W.W. & Company, Inc.

McCormick, Patricia (2002) Cut: Scholastic Inc.

Walsh, Barent W., Rosen, Paul M (1988): Self-Mutilation. Guilford Publications, Inc.

Printed in the United States
97802LV00007B/59/A